J. Krishnamurti taught young people all over the world and founded schools in California, England, and India. "When one is young," he said, "one must be revolutionary, not merely in revolt...to be psychologically revolutionary means non-acceptance of any pattern."

The Dalai Lama calls Krishnamurti "One of the greatest thinkers of the age."

Time magazine named Krishnamurti, along with Mother Teresa, "one of the five saints of the 20th century."

"I feel the meaning of Krishnamurti for our time is that one has to think for oneself and not be swayed by any outside religions or spiritual authorities."

— Van Morrison, Musician

"To listen to him or to read his thoughts is to face oneself and the world with an astonishing morning freshness."

— Anne Morrow Lindbergh, Poet, Author

"In my own life Krishnamurti influenced me profoundly and helped me personally break through the confines of my own self-imposed restrictions to my freedom."

— Deepak Chopra, M.D.

"It was like listening to a discourse of the Buddha—such power, such intrinsic authority."

— Aldous Huxley

WHAT

are you

DOING

with your

LIFE?

J. Krishnamurti

BOOKS ON LIVING FOR TEENAGERS
Volume One

Krishnamurti Publications of America™
OJAI, CALIFORNIA

What Are You Doing with Your Life?: *Books on Living for Teenagers, Volume One* by J. Krishnamurti

Printed in the United States of America.

For information regarding Krishnamurti, contact Krishnamurti Publications of America, P.O. Box 1560, Ojai, CA 93024.

www.kfa.org

Edited by Dale Bick Carlson and Kishore Khairnar
Book design by Jennifer A. Payne
Graphic designs by Carol Nicklaus

Library of Congress Cataloging-in-Publication Data

What are you doing with your life? : teen books on living series.
     p. cm.
  Includes bibliographical references and index.
  ISBN: 1-888004-24-X (alk. paper)
    1. Philosophy. 2. Teenagers--Religious life. 3. Teenagers--
Conduct of life. I. Krishnamurti, J. (Jiddu), 1895-

  B5134.K75 W43 2000
  170'.835--dc21

                     00-020785

CONTENTS

Foreword

Jiddu Krishnamurti (1895-1986) was born of Indian parents, educated in England, and gave talks around the world. He claimed allegiance to no caste, nationality, or religion and was bound by no tradition.

His teachings of more than 20,000,000 words are published in more than 75 books, 700 audiocassettes, and 1200 videocassettes. Thus far, over 4,000,000 copies of books have been sold in twenty-two languages. Together with the Dalai Lama and Mother Teresa, Krishnamurti was declared by *Time* magazine to be one of the five saints of the 20th century.

He traveled the world for sixty-five years speaking spontaneously to large audiences until the end of his life at age ninety. The rejection of all spiritual and psychological authority, including his own, is a fundamental theme. He said man has to free himself of fear, conditioning, authority, and dogma through self-knowledge. He suggested this will bring about order and real psychological change. The conflict-ridden violent world cannot be transformed into a life of goodness, love, and compassion by any political, social, or economic strategies. It can be transformed only through mutation in individuals brought about through their own observation without any guru or organized religion.

Krishnamurti's stature as an original philosopher attracted traditional and non-traditional thinkers and philosophers alike. Heads of state, eminent physicists such as David Bohm, prominent leaders of the United Nations, psychiatrists, psychologists, religious leaders, and university professors engaged in dialogue with Krishnamurti. Students, teachers, and millions of people from all walks of life came to hear him speak and read his books. He bridged science and religion without the use of jargon, so scientists and lay people alike could understand his discussions of time, thought, insight, and death.

He established foundations in the United States, India, England, Canada, Spain, with the defined role of protecting the teachings from being distorted and for disseminating his work, without the authority to interpret or deify the teachings or the person.

In establishing the many schools he founded in India, England, and the United States, Krishnamurti envisioned that education should emphasize the understanding of the mind and heart, not mere academic and intellectual skills; and skills in the art of living, not only the technology to make a living.

Krishnamurti said, "Surely a school is a place where one learns about the totality, the wholeness of life. Academic excellence is absolutely necessary, but a school includes much more than that. It is a place where both the teacher and the taught explore not only the outer world, the world of knowledge, but also their own thinking, their behavior."

He said of his work, "There is no belief demanded or asked, there are no followers, there are no cults, there is no persuasion of any kind, in any direction, and therefore only then we can meet on the same platform, on the same ground, at the same level. Then we can together observe the extraordinary phenomena of human existence."

Kishore Khairnar
Director Sahyadri Study Centre
Krishnamurti Foundation India

Introduction

The way you and I relate to our own brains, to each other, to our own possessions, to money, to work, to sex—these immediate relationships create society. Our relationship to ourselves and one another multiplied by six billion creates the world. The collection of each of our prejudices, all our separate lonelinesses put together, each greedy ambition, each physical or emotional hunger, every anger and sadness in every one of us—we are the world.

The world is not different from us—the world *is* us. So it is simple: if we change, each one of us, we change the world. If even one of us changes, it has a ripple effect. Goodness is contagious.

In school, we are educated to listen to our parents and teachers. Technologically, this makes sense. But thousands of generations have still not learned psychologically how to stop suffering and stop inflicting suffering on others. Psychological evolution has not accompanied biological or scientific evolution. In school, we can all learn how to *make* a living: the *art* of living, however, we must each learn on our own.

Life hurts us all, from loneliness, confusion, the feelings of failure, despair. Life hurts from being poor, emotionally ill, from violence in the streets or at home. We are taught many things, but rarely how to deal with the shock of life's hurts. For one thing, we are not taught that it is not life, but our own reactions to what happens to us that is the cause of pain. It is our fear, rooted in self-protection that causes the pain. To protect the body is natural: but is it natural to protect what we call our 'self?' What is this self that is the root of the trouble, the psychological pain we feel when we try to protect it?

If you merely escape mental pain and confusion with drugs, entertainment, sex, busy-ness, the painful problem is still there, compounded with exhaustion and addiction. Attention to the ways of the self, understanding that fear, desire, and anger are natural but that you don't have to act them out or have everything you want—this insight dissolves mental anguish without adding to it.

We need to learn to understand the self to understand that it is the source of our problems. Not to be self-absorbed, but to pay attention to the thoughts, feelings, activities of the self, its biological and personal, gender and cultural conditioning: this is meditation.

These talks and writings are by a man who lived in the same way as society's great outsiders: the rebel; the wandering poet; the religious philosopher; iconoclastic sage; the breakthrough scientists and psychologists; the great traveling teachers of all millennia. For sixty-five years, Krishnamurti spoke of psychological freedom to whoever would listen to his message. He founded schools for children, teens, young adults, where young people can study all the usual subjects—and themselves as well. In the schools, as in all the talks and writings, he points out that it is not our wars, inner and outer, that will set us free, but the truth about ourselves.

There is no path, no authority, no guru to follow: you have the capacity in yourself to find out what you are, what you are doing with your life, your relationships, and with your work. You must experiment with what is said in this book. Someone else's truth sounds like only opinion until you try it out for yourself. You must look through the microscope yourself, or you will be left with the dust of words, not the actual perception of life.

We are usually taught *what* to think, but not *how* to think. We learn how to escape loneliness and mental suffering, not how to put an end to it.

All of the selections in this volume are taken from Krishnamurti's books, his reported and recorded dialogues, and public talks. Try the experiment of reading this book, and further sources listed in the back, and see for yourself what happens.

A last note: 'K', as this teacher called himself, often apologized to women for using the words 'he', 'him', 'his', 'man', in the talks and writings. He included all human beings in his teachings.

Dale Carlson
Editor

SECTION ONE

Your Self and Your Life

CHAPTER ONE

What Are You?

— 1 —

Understanding the Mind

It seems to me that without understanding the way our minds work, one cannot understand and resolve the very complex problems of living. This understanding cannot come through book knowledge. The mind is, in itself, quite a complex problem. In the very process of understanding one's own mind, the crisis which each one of us faces in life can perhaps be understood and gone beyond.

— 2 —

It seems to me that it is very important to understand the process of our own minds...

— 3 —
What Is the Mind?

We do not know the workings of our own mind—the mind as it is, not as it should be or as we would like it to be. The mind is the only instrument we have, the instrument with which we think, we act, in which we have our being. If we do not understand that mind in operation as it is functioning in each one of us, any problem that we are confronted with will become more complex and more destructive. So it seems to me, to understand one's mind is the first essential function of all education.

What is our mind, yours and mine?—not according to...someone else. If you do not follow my description of the mind, but actually, while listening to me, observe your own mind in operation, then perhaps it would be profitable and worthwhile to go into the whole question of thought. What is our mind? It is the result, is it not, of climate, of centuries of tradition, the so-called culture, the social and economic influences, the environment, the ideas, the dogmas that society imprints on the mind through religion, through so-called knowledge and superficial information. Please observe your own mind, and not merely follow the description that I am giving because the description has very little significance. If we can watch the operations of our mind, then perhaps we shall be able to deal with the problems of life as they concern us.

The mind is divided into the conscious and the unconscious. If we do not like to use these two words, we might use the terms, superficial and hidden—the superficial parts of the mind and the deeper layers of the mind. The whole of the conscious as well as the unconscious, the superficial as well as the hidden, the total process of our thinking—only part of which we are conscious of, and the rest, which is the major part, we are not conscious of—is what we call consciousness. This consciousness is time, is the result of centuries of man's endeavor.

We are made to believe in certain ideas from childhood, we are conditioned by dogmas, by beliefs, by theories. Each one of us is conditioned by various influences, and from that conditioning, from those limited and unconscious influences, our thoughts spring and take the form of a Communist, a Hindu, a Muslim, or a scientist. Thought obviously springs from the background of memory, of tradition, and it is with this background of both the conscious as well as the unconscious, the superficial as well as the deeper layers of the mind, that we meet life. Life is always in movement, never static. But, our minds are static. Our minds are conditioned, held, tethered to dogma, to belief, to experience, to knowledge. With this tethered mind, with this mind that is so conditioned, so heavily held, we meet life, which is in constant movement. Life, with its many complex and swiftly changing problems, is never still, and it requires a fresh approach every day, every minute. So, when we meet this life, there is a constant struggle between the mind that is conditioned and static, and life that is in constant movement. That is what is happening, is it not?

There is not only a conflict between life and the conditioned mind, but such a mind, meeting life, creates more problems. We acquire superficial knowledge, new ways of conquering nature, science. But the mind that has acquired knowledge still remains in the conditioned state, bound to a particular form of belief.

So, our problem is not how to meet life, but how can the mind, with all its conditioning, with its dogmas, beliefs, free itself? It is only the free mind that can meet life, not the mind that is tethered to any system, to any belief, to any particular knowledge. So is it not important, if we would not create more problems, if we would put an end to misery, sorrow, to understand the workings of our own minds?

— 4 —
What Is the Self?

Do we know what we mean by the self? By that, I mean the idea, the memory, the conclusion, the experience, the various forms of nameable and unnameable intentions, the conscious endeavor to be or not to be, the accumulated memory of the unconscious, the racial, the group, the individual, the clan, and the whole of it all, whether it is projected outwardly in action or projected spiritually as virtue; the striving after all this is the self. In it is included the competition, the desire to be. The whole process of that is the self; and we know actually when we are faced with it that it is an evil thing. I am using the word 'evil' intentionally, because the self is dividing: the self is self-enclosing: its activities, however noble, are separative and isolating. We know all this. We also know those extraordinary moments when the self is not there, in which there is no sense of endeavor, of effort, and which happens when there is love.

— 5 —

Self-Knowledge Is a Process

So, to understand the innumerable problems that each one of us has, is it not essential that there be self-knowledge? And that is one of the most difficult things, self-awareness— which does not mean an isolation, a withdrawal. Obviously, to know oneself is essential; but to know oneself does not imply a withdrawal from relationship. And it would be a mistake, surely, to think that one can know oneself significantly, completely, fully, through isolation, through exclusion, or by going to some psychologist, or to some priest; or that one can learn self-knowledge through a book. Self-knowledge is obviously a process, not an end in itself; and to know oneself, one must be aware of oneself in action, which is relationship. You discover yourself, not in isolation, not in withdrawal, but in relationship—in relationship to society, to your wife, your husband, your brother, to man; but to discover how you react, what your responses are, requires an extraordinary alertness of mind, a keenness of perception.

— 6 —

What You Are, the World Is

What is the relationship between yourself and the misery, the confusion, in and around you? Surely this confusion, this misery, did not come into being by itself. You and I have created it, not a capitalist nor a communist nor a fascist society, but you and I have created it in our relationship with each other. What you are within has been projected without, onto the world; what you are, what you think and what you feel, what you do in your everyday existence, is projected outwardly, and that constitutes the world. If we are miserable, confused, chaotic within, by projection that becomes the world, that becomes society, because the relationship between yourself and myself, between myself and another is society—society is the product of our relationship —and if our relationship is confused, egocentric, narrow, limited, national, we project that and bring chaos into the world.

What you are, the world is. So your problem is the world's problem. Surely, this is a simple and basic fact, is it not? In our relationship with the one or the many we seem somehow to overlook this point all the time. We want to bring about alteration through a system or through a revolution in ideas or values based on a system, forgetting that it is you and I who create society, who bring about confusion or order by the way in which we live. So we must begin near, that is, we must concern ourselves with our daily existence, with our daily thoughts and feelings and actions which are revealed in the manner of earning our livelihood and in our relationship with ideas or beliefs.

— 7 —

Your Struggle Is the Human Struggle

A total, an enriching revolution cannot take place unless you and I understand ourselves as a total process. You and I are not isolated individuals but are the result of the whole human struggle with its illusions, fancies, pursuits, ignorance, strife, conflict, and misery. One cannot begin to alter the condition of the world without understanding oneself. If you see that, there is immediately within you a complete revolution, is there not? Then no guru is necessary because knowledge of oneself is from moment to moment, it is not the accumulation of hearsay, nor is it contained in the precepts of religious teachers. Because you are discovering yourself in relationship with another from moment to moment, relationship has a completely different meaning.

Relationship then is a revelation, a constant process of the discovery of oneself, and from this self-discovery, action takes place.

So, self-knowledge can come only through relationship, not through isolation. Relationship is action, and self-knowledge is the result of awareness in action.

— 8 —

Transform Yourself and You Transform the World

The transformation of the world is brought about by the transformation of oneself, because the self is the product and a part of the total process of human existence. To transform oneself, self-knowledge is essential; without knowing what you are, there is no basis for right thought, and without knowing yourself, there cannot be transformation.

— 9 —

Why Change Now?

There is no essential difference between the old and the young, for both are slaves to their own desires and gratifications. Maturity is not a matter of age; it comes with understanding. The ardent spirit of inquiry is perhaps easier for the young, because those who are older have been battered about by life, conflicts have worn them out and death in different forms awaits them. This does not mean that they are incapable of purposive inquiry, but only that it is more difficult for them. Many adults are immature and rather childish, and this is a contributing cause of the confusion and misery in the world. It is the older people who are responsible for the prevailing economic and moral crisis; and one of our unfortunate weaknesses is that we want someone else to act for us and change the course of our lives. We wait for others to revolt and build anew, and we remain inactive until we are assured of the outcome. It is security and success that most of us are after; and a mind that is seeking security, that craves success, is not intelligent, and is therefore incapable of integrated action. There can be integrated action only if one is aware of one's own conditioning, of one's racial, national, political, and religious prejudices; that is, only if one realizes that the ways of the self are ever separative.

Life is a well of deep waters. One can come to it with small buckets and draw only a little water, or one can come with large vessels, drawing plentiful waters that will nourish and sustain. While one is young is the time to investigate, to experiment with everything. The school should help its young people to discover their vocations and responsibilities, and not merely cram their minds with facts and technical knowledge. It should be the soil in which they can grow without fear, happily and integrally.

— 10 —

Thought Cannot Solve the Problem of the Self

The more we think over a problem, the more we investigate, analyze, and discuss it, the more complex it becomes. So is it possible to look at the problem comprehensively, wholly? How is this possible? Because that, it seems to me, is our major difficulty. Our problems are being multiplied—there is imminent danger of war, there is every kind of disturbance in our relationships—and how can we understand all that comprehensively, as a whole? Obviously it can be solved only when we can look at it as a whole—not in compartments, not divided. When is that possible? Surely it is only possible when the process of thinking—which has its source in the 'me', the self, in the background of tradition, of conditioning, of prejudice, of hope, of despair—has come to an end. Can we understand this self, not by analyzing, but by seeing the thing as it is, being aware of it as a fact and not as a theory?—not seeking to dissolve the self in order to achieve a result but seeing the activity of the self, the 'me', constantly in action. Can we *look* at it, without any movement to destroy or to encourage? That is the problem, is it not? If, in each one of us, the center of the 'me' is non-existent, with its desire for power, position, authority, continuance, self-preservation, surely our problems will come to an end!

The self is a problem that thought cannot resolve. There must be an awareness which is not of thought. To be aware, without condemnation or justification, of the activities of the self—just to be aware—is sufficient. If you are aware in order to find out *how* to resolve the problem, in order to transform it, in order to produce a result, then it is still within the field of the self, of the 'me'. So long as we are seeking a result, whether through analysis, through awareness, through constant examination of every thought, we are still within the field of thought, which is within the field of the 'me', of the 'I', of the ego, or what you will.

As long as the activity of the mind exists, surely there can be no love. When there is love, we shall have no social problems.

CHAPTER TWO
What Do You Want?

— I —

Security, Happiness, Pleasure

What is it that most of us are seeking? What is it that each one of us wants? Especially in this restless world, where everybody is trying to find some kind of peace, some kind of happiness, a refuge, surely it is important to find out, isn't it, what it is that we are trying to seek, what it is that we are trying to discover? Probably most of us are seeking some kind of happiness, some kind of peace; in a world that is ridden with turmoil, wars, contention, strife, we want a refuge where there can be some peace. I think that is what most of us want. So we pursue, go from one leader to another, from one religious organization to another, from one teacher to another.

Now, is it that we are seeking happiness or is it that we are seeking gratification of some kind from which we hope to derive happiness? There is a difference between happiness and gratification. Can you *seek* happiness? Perhaps you can find gratification but surely you cannot *find* happiness. Happiness is derivative; it is a by-product of something else. So, before we give our minds and hearts to something which demands a great deal of earnestness, attention, thought, care, we must find out, must we not, what it is that we are seeking; whether it is happiness, or gratification? I am afraid most of us are seeking gratification. We want to be gratified, we want to find a sense of fullness at the end of our search.

After all, if one is seeking peace one can find it very easily. One can devote oneself blindly to some kind of cause, to an idea, and take shelter there. Surely that does not solve the problem. Mere isolation in an enclosing idea is not a release from conflict. So we must find, must we not, what it is—inwardly, as well as outwardly—that each one of us wants? If we are clear on that matter, then we don't have to go anywhere, to any teacher, to any church, to any organization. Therefore our difficulty is, to be clear in ourselves regarding our intention, is it not? Can we be clear? And does this clarity come through searching, through trying to find out what others say, from the highest teacher to the ordinary preacher in a church around the corner? Have you got to go to somebody to find out? Yet that is what we are doing, is it not? We read innumerable books, we attend many meetings and discuss, we join various organizations trying thereby to find a remedy to the conflict, to the miseries in our lives. Or, if we don't do all that, we think we have found; that is, we say that a particular organization, a particular teacher, a particular book satisfies us; we have found everything we want in that; and we remain in that, crystallized and enclosed.

Do we not seek, through all this confusion, something permanent, something lasting, something which we call real, God, truth, what you like—the name doesn't matter, the word is not the thing, surely. So don't let us be caught in words. Leave that to the professional lecturers. There is a search for something permanent, is there not, in most of us? —something we can cling to, something which will give us assurance, a hope, a lasting enthusiasm, a lasting certainty, because in ourselves we are so uncertain. We do not know ourselves. We know a lot about facts, what the books have said; but we do not know for ourselves, we do not have a direct experience.

And what is it that we call permanent? What is it that we are seeking, which will, or which we hope will give us permanency? Are we not seeking lasting happiness, lasting gratification, lasting certainty? We want something that will endure everlastingly, which will gratify us. If we strip ourselves of all the words and phrases, and actually look at it, this is what we want. We want permanent pleasure...

— 2 —

Happiness Cannot Be Pursued

What do you mean by happiness? Some will say happiness consists of getting what you want. You want a car, and you get it, and you are happy. I want a sari or clothes; I want to go to Europe, and if I can, I am happy. I want to be the...greatest politician, and if I get it, I am happy; if I cannot get it, I am unhappy. So what you call happiness is getting what you want, achievement or success, becoming noble, getting anything that you want. As long as you want something and you can get it, you feel perfectly happy; you are not frustrated. But, if you cannot get what you want, then unhappiness begins. All of us are concerned with this, not only the rich and the poor. The rich and the poor all want to get something for themselves, for their family, for society; and if they are prevented, stopped, they will be unhappy. We are not discussing, we are not saying that the poor should not have what they want. That is not the problem. We are trying to find out what is happiness and whether happiness is something of which you are conscious. The moment you are conscious that you are happy, that you have much, is that happiness? The moment you are conscious that you are happy, it is not happiness, is it? So you cannot go after happiness. The moment you are conscious that you are humble, you are not humble. So happiness is not a thing to be pursued; it comes. But if you seek it, it will evade you.

— 3 —

Pleasure, Enjoyment, Turns into Dependency and Fear of Loss

We do not really enjoy anything. We look at it, we are superficially amused or excited by it, we have a sensation which we call joy. But enjoyment is something far deeper, which must be understood and gone into.

When we are young, we enjoy and take delight in things—in games, in clothes, in reading a book or writing a poem or painting a picture, or in pushing each other about...As we grow older, although we still want to enjoy things, the best has gone out of us; we prefer other kinds of sensations—passion, lust, power, position.

— 4 —

As we grow older, the things of life lose their meaning; our minds become dull, insensitive, and so, we try to enjoy, we try to force ourselves to look at pictures, to look at trees, to look at little children playing. We read some sacred book or other and try to find its meaning, its depth, its significance. But, it is all an effort, a travail, something to struggle with.

I think it is very important to understand this thing called joy, the enjoyment of things. When you see something very beautiful, you want to possess it, you want to hold onto it, you want to call it your own—it is *my* tree, *my* bird, *my* house, *my* husband, *my* wife. We want to hold it, and in that very process of holding, the thing that you once enjoyed is gone because in the very holding there is dependence, there is fear, there is exclusion, and so the thing that gave joy, a sense of inward beauty, is lost, and life becomes enclosed…

To know real joy, one must go much deeper.

— 5 —

Joy Is the Absence of the 'Me' that Wants

We may move from one refinement to another, from one subtlety to another, from one enjoyment to another, but at the center of it all there is the 'me'—the 'me' that is enjoying, that wants more happiness, the 'me' that searches, looks for, longs for happiness, the 'me' that struggles, the 'me' that becomes more and more "refined," but never likes to come to an end. It is only when the 'me' in all its subtle forms comes to an end that there is a state of bliss which cannot be sought after, an ecstasy, a real joy, without pain, without corruption. Now, in all our joy, all our happiness, is corruption; because behind it there is pain, behind it there is fear.

When the mind goes beyond the thought of the 'me', the experiencer, the observer, the thinker, then there is a possibility of happiness which is incorruptible. That happiness cannot be made permanent, in the sense in which we use that word. But, our mind is seeking permanent happiness, something that will last, that will continue. That very desire for continuity is corruption. But when the mind is free from the 'me', there is a happiness, from moment to moment, which comes without your seeking, in which there is no gathering, no storing up, no putting by of happiness. It is not something which you can hold on to.

— 6 —

We Want Security

There is the desire for security. And one can understand this desire to be secure when you meet a wild animal, a snake; or you watch when you cross the road. But there is no other form of security. Really, if you look at it, there is no other form. You would like to have security with your wife, children, neighbor, your relations—if you have relations—but you don't have it. You may have your mother, you may have your father, but you are not related, you are completely isolated—we will go into that. There is no security, psychological security, at any time, at any level, with anybody—this is the most difficult thing to realize. There is no psychological security with another because he is a human being, and so are you; he is free, and so are you. But we want security in our relationships, through marriage, through vows—you know the tricks we play upon ourselves and upon others. This is an obvious fact; it does not need great analysis.

— 7 —

Realizing the Fact of Insecurity

We never come into contact with this insecurity. We are afraid of being completely insecure. It requires a great deal of intelligence to understand that insecurity. When one feels completely insecure, one runs away. Or, not finding security in anything, one becomes unbalanced, ready to commit suicide, to go to a mental hospital, or one becomes a most devout religious person—which are all the same, forms of imbalance. To realize—not intellectually, not verbally, not as a determined, willed attitude—the fact that there is no security requires an extraordinarily simple, clear, harmonious living.

— 8 —

Why Are We Seeking Something?

We are endlessly seeking, and we never ask why we are seeking. The obvious answer is that we are dissatisfied, unhappy, unfortunate, lonely, unloved, fearful. We need something to cling to, we need somebody to protect us—the father, the mother, and so on—and so we are seeking. When we are seeking, we are always finding. Unfortunately, we will always find when we are seeking.

So the first thing is not to seek. You understand? You all have been told that you must seek, experiment with truth, find out truth, go after it, pursue it, chase it, and that you must discipline, control yourself. And then somebody comes along and says, "Don't do all that. Don't seek at all." Naturally, your reaction is either to ask him to go away or you turn your back, or you find out for yourself why he says such a thing—not accept, not deny, but question. And what are you seeking?

Inquire about yourself. You are seeking; you are saying that you are missing something in this life inwardly—not at the level of technique or having a petty job or more money. What is it that we are seeking? We are seeking because in us there is such deep dissatisfaction with our family, with society, with culture, with our own selves, and we want to satisfy, to go beyond this gnawing discontent that is destroying. And why are we discontented? I know discontent can very easily be satisfied. Give a young man who has been discontented—

a communist or a revolutionary—a good job, and he forgets all about it. Give him a nice house, a nice car, a nice garden, a good position, and you will see that discontent disappears. If he can achieve an ideological success, that discontent disappears too. But you never ask why you are discontented—not the people who have jobs, and who want better jobs. We must understand the root cause of discontent before we can examine the whole structure and the meaning of pleasure and, therefore, of sorrow.

CHAPTER THREE

Thought, the Thinker, and the Prison of the Self

— I —

The Thinker and Thought

Is there any relationship between the thinker and his thought, or is there only thought and not a thinker? If there are no thoughts there is no thinker. When you have thoughts, is there a thinker? Perceiving the impermanency of thoughts, thought itself creates the thinker who gives himself permanency; so thought creates the thinker; then the thinker establishes himself as a permanent entity apart from thoughts which are always in a state of flux. So, thought creates the thinker and not the other way about. The thinker does not create thought, for if there are no thoughts, there is no thinker. The thinker separates himself from his parent and tries to establish a relationship—a relationship between the so-called permanent, which is the thinker created by thought, and the impermanent or transient, which is thought. So, both are really transient.

Pursue a thought completely to its very end. Think it out fully, feel it out and discover for yourself what happens. You will find that there is no thinker at all. For, when thought ceases, the thinker is not. We think there are two states, as the thinker and the thought. These two states are fictitious, unreal. There is only thought, and the bundle of thought creates the 'me', the thinker.

— 2 —

Thought Is the Response of Stored-Up
Memory: Race, Group, Family

What do we mean by thought? When do you think? Obviously, thought is the result of a response, neurological or psychological, the response of stored-up memory. There is the immediate response of the nerves to a sensation, and there is the psychological response of stored-up memory, the influence of race, group, guru, family, tradition, and so on—

all of which you call thought. So, the thought process is the response of memory, is it not? You would have no thoughts if you had no memory, and the response of memory to a certain experience brings the thought process into action.

— 3 —

What Is the Origin of Thinking?

One can see very simply that all thinking is a reaction to the past—the past being memory, knowledge, experience. All thinking is the result of the past. The past—which is time, yesterday and that yesterday stretching out indefinitely into the past—is what is considered time: time as the past, time as the present, time as the future. Time has been divided into these three parts, and time is like a river, flowing. We have divided into these fragments, and in these fragments thought is caught.

— 4 —

Memory as Thought Has Its Place

We are not saying that thought must stop; thought has a definite function. Without thought we couldn't go to the office, we wouldn't know where we live, we wouldn't be able to function at all.

But if we would bring about a radical revolution in the whole of consciousness, in the very structure of thinking, we must realize that thought, having built this society, with all its mess, cannot possibly resolve it.

— 5 —

Thought Seeks Security

Thought is the very essence of security, and that is what the most bourgeois mind wants—security, security at every level! To bring about a total change of the human consciousness, thought must function at one level and must not function at another level. Thought must function naturally, normally at one level, the everyday level—physically, technologically—with knowledge, but must not overflow into another field where thought has no reality at all. If I had no thought I wouldn't be able to speak. But a radical change within myself as a human being cannot be brought about through thought, because thought can only function in relation to conflict. Thought can only breed conflict.

— 6 —

Why Change?

Man has lived for two million years or more, but he has not solved the problem of sorrow. He is always sorrow-ridden: he has sorrow as his shadow or as his companion. Sorrow of losing somebody; sorrow in not being able to fulfill his ambitions, his greed, his energy; sorrow of physical pain; sorrow of psychological anxiety; sorrow of guilt; sorrow of hope and despair—that has been the lot of man; that has been the lot of every human being. And he has always tried to solve this problem—to end sorrow within the field of consciousness— by trying to avoid it, by running away from sorrow, by suppressing it, by identifying himself with something greater than himself, by taking to drink, to women, by doing everything in order to avoid this anxiety, this pain, this despair, this immense loneliness and boredom of life—which is always within this field of consciousness, which is the result of time.

— 7 —

Sorrow Cannot Be Ended through Thought

So man has always exercised thought as a means to get rid of sorrow by right effort, by right thinking, by living morally, and so on. The exercise of thought has been his guide—thought with intellect, and all the rest of it. But thought is the result of time, and time is this consciousness.

Whatever you do within the field of this consciousness, sorrow can never end. Whether you go to the temple, or you take to drink, both are the same. So, if there is learning, one sees that through thought there is no possibility of a radical change, but there will be continuity of sorrow. If one sees that, then one can move in a different dimension. I am using the word *see* in the sense not intellectually, not verbally, but with a total understanding of this fact—the fact that sorrow cannot be ended through thought.

— 8 —

Living with What Is

That is, is it possible to look at it without thought? This does not mean that you go blank, but you look at it. And it is only possible to look when there is no sense of the 'me' interfering with the look. You understand? That is, there is the fact that I am violent. And I have pushed away from me the silly idea of not being violent, as that is too juvenile, too absurd, and has no meaning. *What is* is the fact—that I am violent. And also I see that to struggle to get rid of it, to bring about a change in it, needs effort, and that the very effort which is exercised is a part of violence. And yet, I realize that violence must be completely changed, transformed; there must be a mutation in that.

Now, how is it to be done? If you just push it aside because this subject is very difficult, you will miss an extraordinary state of life: existence without effort, and therefore, a life of the highest sensitivity, which is the highest intelligence. And it is only this extraordinarily heightened intelligence that can discover the limits and the measure of time, and can go beyond that. Do you understand the question, the problem? So far, we have used the ideal as a means or as an incentive to get rid of *what is*, and that breeds contradiction, hypocrisy, hardness, brutality. And if we push that ideal aside, then we are left with the fact. Then we see that the fact must be altered, and that it must be altered without the least friction. Any friction, any struggle, any effort, destroys the sensitivity of the mind and the heart.

So what is one to do? What one comes to do is to observe the fact—to observe the fact without any translation, interpretation, identification, condemnation, evaluation—just to observe.

— 9 —

The Nature of Observation

You know, I was told that an electron, measured by an instrument, behaves in one way—which cannot be measured on the graph. But when that same electron is observed by the human eye through a microscope, that very observation by the human mind, through the microscope, alters the behavior of that electron. That is, the human watching the electron brings about in the electron itself a different behavior, and that behavior is different from the behavior when the human mind is not observing it.

When you just observe the fact, then you will see that there is a different behavior, as there is when the electron is observed. When you look at the fact without any pressure, then that fact undergoes a complete mutation, a complete change, without effort.

— 10 —

Loneliness: Living Only in the Prison Of 'Me'

And there is the sorrow of loneliness. I do not know if you have ever been lonely: when you suddenly realize that you have no relationship with anybody...And this loneliness is a form of death. As we said, there is dying not only when life comes to an end but when there is no answer, there is no way out. That is also a form of death: being in the prison of your own self-centered activity, endlessly. When you are caught in your own thoughts, in your own agony, in your own superstitions, in your deadly, daily routine of habit and thoughtlessness, that is also death—not just the ending of the body.

And how to end it also one must find out...The ending of sorrow is possible.

— II —
Awareness

So I think our inquiry must be not for the solution of our immediate problems but rather to find out whether the mind—the conscious as well as the deep unconscious mind in which is stored all the tradition, the memories, the inheritance of racial knowledge—whether all of it can be put aside. I think it can be done only if the mind is capable of being aware without any sense of demand, without any pressure— just to be aware. I think it is one of the most difficult things—to be so aware—because we are caught in the immediate problem and in its immediate solution, and so our lives are very superficial.

— 12 —
Right Thinking and Awareness

Right thought and right thinking are two different states. Right thought is merely a conformity to a pattern, to a system. Right thought is static; it involves the constant friction of choice. Right thinking or true thinking is to be discovered. It cannot be learned. It cannot be practiced. Right thinking is a movement of self-knowledge from moment to moment. This movement of self-knowledge exists in the awareness of relationship...

Right thinking can only come into being when there is awareness of every thought and feeling, the awareness not only of a particular group of thoughts and feelings, but of all thoughts and feelings.

— 13 —
Thought Can Never Be Free

So we must understand very clearly that our thinking is the response of memory, and memory is mechanistic. Knowledge is ever incomplete, and all thinking born of knowledge is limited, partial, never free. So there is no freedom of thought. But we can begin to discover a freedom which is not a process of thought, and in which the mind is simply aware of all its conflicts and of all the influences impinging on it.

CHAPTER FOUR

Insight, Intelligence, and Revolution in Your Life

— I —

Intellect Is not Intelligence

Training the intellect does not result in intelligence. Rather, intelligence comes into being when one acts in perfect harmony, both intellectually and emotionally. There is a vast distinction between intellect and intelligence. Intellect is merely thought functioning independently of emotion. When intellect, irrespective of emotion, is trained in any particular direction, one may have great intellect, but one does not have intelligence, because in intelligence there is the inherent capacity to feel as well as to reason; in intelligence both capacities are equally present, intensely and harmoniously.

Now modern education is developing the intellect, offering more and more explanations of life, more and more theories, without the harmonious quality of affection. Therefore we have developed cunning minds to escape from conflict; hence we are satisfied with explanations that scientists and philosophers give us. The mind—the intellect—is satisfied with these innumerable explanations, but intelligence is not, for to understand there must be complete unity of mind and heart in action...

Until you really approach all of life with your intelligence, instead of merely with your intellect, no system in the world will save man from the ceaseless toil for bread.

— 2 —

Intelligence, Awareness May Burn Away the Problems

All thinking obviously is conditioned; there is no such thing as free thinking. Thinking can never be free, it is the outcome of our conditioning, of our background, of our culture, of our climate, of our social, economic, political background. The very books that you read and the very practices that you do are all established in the background, and any thinking must be the result of that background. So if we can be aware—and we can go presently into what it signifies, what it means, to be aware—perhaps we shall be able to uncondition the mind without the process of will, without the determination to uncondition the mind. Because the moment you determine, there is an entity who wishes, an entity who says, "I must uncondition my mind." That entity itself is the outcome of our desire to achieve a certain result, so a conflict is already there. So, is it possible to be aware of our conditioning, just to be aware?—in which there is no conflict at all. That very awareness, if allowed, may perhaps burn away the problems.

— 3 —

Understanding Comes when the Brain Is Quiet

Now, when do you understand, when is there understanding? I do not know if you have noticed that there is understanding when the mind is very quiet, even for a second; there is the flash of understanding when verbalization of thought is not. Just experiment with it and you will see for yourself that you have the flash of understanding, that extraordinary rapidity of insight, when mind is very still, when thought is absent, when the mind is not burdened with its noise. So, the understanding of anything—of a modern picture, of a child, of your wife, of your neighbor, or the understanding of truth which is in all things—can only come when the mind is very still. But such stillness cannot be cultivated because if you cultivate a still mind, it is not a still mind, it is a dead mind.

It is essential to have a still mind, a quiet mind, in order to understand, which is fairly obvious to those who have experimented with all this. The more you are interested in something, the more your intention to understand, the more simple, clear, free the mind is Then verbalization ceases. After all, thought is word, and it is the word that interferes. It is the screen of words, which is memory, that intervenes between the challenge and the response. It is the word that is responding to the challenge, which we call intellection. So, the mind that is chattering, that is verbalizing, cannot understand truth—truth in relationship, not an abstract truth. There is no abstract truth. But truth is very subtle. It is the subtlety that is difficult to follow. It is not abstract. It comes so swiftly, so darkly, it cannot be held by the mind. Like a thief in the night, it comes darkly, not when you are prepared to receive it. Your reception is merely an invitation of greed.

So, a mind that is caught in the net of words cannot understand truth.

— 4 —

Intelligence Is Crippled by Analysis

The very first thing to do, if I may suggest it, is to find out why you are thinking in a certain way, and why you are feeling in a certain manner. Don't try to alter it, don't try to analyze your thoughts and your emotions; but become conscious of why you are thinking in a particular groove and from what motive you act. Although you can discover the motive through analysis, although you may find out something through analysis, it will not be real; it will be real only when you are intensely aware at the moment of the functioning of your thought and emotion; then you will see their extraordinary subtlety, their fine delicacy. So long as you have a "must" and a "must not," in this compulsion you will never discover that swift wandering of thought and emotion. And I am sure you have been brought up in the school of "must" and "must not" and hence you have destroyed thought and feeling. You have been bound and crippled by systems, methods, by your teachers. So leave all those "must" and "must nots." This does not mean that there shall be licentiousness, but become aware of a mind that is ever saying, "I must," and "I must not." Then as a flower blossoms forth of a morning, so intelligence happens, is there, functioning, creating comprehension.

— 5 —

Freedom from the Self

To free the mind from all conditioning, you must see the totality of it without thought. This is not a conundrum; experiment with it and you will see. Do you ever see anything without thought? Have you ever listened, looked, without bringing in this whole process of reaction? You will say that it is impossible to see without thought; you will say no mind can be unconditioned. When you say that, you have already blocked yourself by thought, for the fact is you do not know.

So can I look, can the mind be aware of its conditioning? I think it can. Please experiment. Can you be aware that you are a Hindu, a Socialist, a communist, this or that, just be aware without saying that it is right or wrong? Because it is such a difficult task just to see, we say it is impossible. I say it is only when you are aware of this totality of your being without any reaction that the conditioning goes, totally, deeply—which is really the freedom from the self.

— 6 —

Ignorance Is Lack of Self-Knowledge

Ignorance is lack of knowledge of the ways of the self, and this ignorance cannot be dissipated by superficial activities and reforms; it can be dissipated by one's constant awareness of the movements and responses of the self in all its relationships.

What we must realize is that we are not only conditioned by environment, but that we *are* the environment—we are not something apart from it. Our thoughts and responses are conditioned by the values which society, of which we are a part, has imposed upon us.

— 7 —

Our Human Brain Took a Wrong Turn, Seeing Separation between the Self and the Not-Self

We never see that we are the total environment because there are several entities in us, all revolving around the 'me', the self. The self is made up of these entities, which are merely desires in various forms. From this conglomeration of desires arises the central figure, the thinker, the will of the 'me' and the 'mine'; and a division is thus established between the self and the not-self, between the 'me' and the environment or society. This separation is the beginning of conflict, inward and outward.

Awareness of this whole process, both the conscious and the hidden, is meditation; and through this meditation the self, with its desires and conflicts, is transcended. Self-knowledge is necessary if one is to be free of the influences and values that give shelter to the self; and in this freedom alone is there creation, truth, God, or what you will.

Opinion and tradition mold our thoughts and feelings from the tenderest age. The immediate influences and impressions produce an effect which is powerful and lasting, and which shapes the whole course of our conscious and unconscious life. Conformity begins in childhood through education and the impact of society.

The desire to imitate is a very strong factor in our life, not only at the superficial levels, but also profoundly. We have hardly any independent thoughts and feelings. When they do occur, they are mere reactions, and are therefore not free from the established pattern; for there is no freedom in reaction...

When we are inwardly dependent, then tradition has a great hold on us, and a mind that thinks along traditional lines cannot discover that which is new. By conforming we become mediocre imitators, cogs in a cruel social machine. It is what we think that matters, not what others *want* us to think. When we conform to tradition, we soon become mere copies of what we should be.

This imitation of what we should be, breeds fear; and fear kills creative thinking. Fear dulls the mind and heart so that we are not alert to the whole significance of life; we become insensitive to our own sorrows, to the movement of the birds, to the smiles and miseries of others.

— 8 —

Knowledge, Wisdom, Intelligence

Knowledge is not comparable with intelligence, knowledge is not wisdom. Wisdom is not marketable, it is not a merchandise that can be bought with the price of learning or discipline. Wisdom cannot be found in books; it cannot be accumulated, memorized or stored up. Wisdom comes with the abnegation of the self. To have an open mind is more important than learning; and we can have an open mind, not by cramming it full of information, but by being aware of our own thoughts and feelings, by carefully observing ourselves and the influences about us, by listening to others, by watching the rich and the poor, the powerful and the lowly. Wisdom does not come through fear and oppression, but through the observation and understanding of everyday incidents in human relationship...

Intelligence is much greater than intellect, for it is the integration of reason and love; but there can be intelligence only when there is self-knowledge, the deep understanding of the total process of oneself...We must be aware of our conditioning and its responses, both collective and personal.

It is only when one is fully aware of the activities of the self with its contradictory desires and pursuits, its hopes and fears, that there is a possibility of going beyond the self.

Only love and right thinking will bring about true revolution, the revolution within ourselves.

CHAPTER FIVE

Escape; Entertainment; Pleasure

— I —

Technology Produces More and More Leisure

Man is having more and more leisure through automation, through the development of cybernetics, through electronic brains, and so on. And that leisure is going to be used either for entertainment—religious entertainment or entertainment through various forms of amusements—or for more and more destructive purposes in relationship between man and man; or, having that leisure, he is going to turn inwardly. There are only these three possibilities. Technologically he can go to the moon, but that will not solve the human problem. Nor will the mere use of his leisure for a religious or some other amusement solve it. Going to church or temple, beliefs, dogmas, reading sacred books—all that is really a form of amusement. Or, man will go deeply into himself and question every value that man has created through the centuries, and try to find out if there is something more than the mere product of the brain. There are whole groups of people, throughout the world, that are revolting against the established order by taking various forms of drugs, denying any form of activity in society, and so on.

Please, I have not taken any drug, because to me any form of stimulant—any form, listening to the speaker and therefore being stimulated, or drink, or sex, or a drug, or going to mass and getting into a certain state of emotional tension—is utterly detrimental, because any stimulant in any form, however subtle, makes the mind dull, because it depends on that stimulant. The stimulant establishes a certain habit and makes the mind dull.

— 2 —

Escapes Are the Desire to Forget Ourselves

All our conflicts, all our ambitions, are very small, very petty. So, we want to identify ourselves with something. If it is not God, it is the state,…the government, the people who rule, the society. If it is not that, it is utopia, something very far away, a marvelous society that we are going to build; in the building of it you destroy many people, but that does not really matter to you. If you do not believe in any of these, you believe in having a good time and forget yourself in material things. Such a person is called materialistic, and the man who forgets himself in the spiritual world is called spiritual. Both of them have the same intention—one to forget himself in cinemas and the other in books, in rituals, in sitting on the banks of a river meditating, in renunciation— not to have any burden, to lose oneself in some kind of action, to lose oneself in the worship of something. So, there is the desire to lose oneself because one feels very small. The self may not be small to you when you are young. But, as you grow older, you will see how little substance there is in it, how little value it has; it is like a shadow, with few qualities, full of struggles, pains, sorrows, and that is all. So one soon gets bored with it and pursues something else in order to forget oneself. That is what all of us are doing. The rich want to forget themselves in night clubs, in amusements, in cars, in traveling. The clever ones want to forget themselves, so they begin to invent, to have extraordinary beliefs. The stupid ones want to forget themselves, and so they follow people, they have gurus who tell them what to do. The ambitious ones also want to forget themselves in doing something. So, all of us, as we mature, as we grow older, want to forget ourselves, and so we try to find something greater with which to be identified.

— 3 —

Escape from What Is *Makes for Slavery*

To escape collectively is the highest form of security. In facing *what is*, we can do something about it; but to take flight from *what is* inevitably makes us stupid and dull, slaves to sensation and confusion.

— 4 —

Dependence Indicates the Emptiness of Our Lives

It is the desire for sensation that makes us cling to music, possess beauty. Dependence on outward line and form only indicates the emptiness of our own being, which we fill with music, art, with deliberate silence. It is because this unvarying emptiness is filled or covered over with sensations that there is the everlasting fear of *what is*, of what we are. Sensations have a beginning and an end, they can be repeated and expanded; but experiencing is not within the limits of time. What is essential is experiencing, which is denied in the pursuit of sensation. Sensations are limited, personal, they cause conflict and misery; but experiencing, which is wholly different from the repetition of an experience, is without continuity. Only in experiencing is there renewal, transformation.

— 5 —

Why Is Sex the Most Universal Escape?

Why is it that sex has become such a problem in our lives? Let us go into it, not with constraint, not with anxiety, fear, condemnation. Why has it become a problem? Surely, for most of you it is a problem. Why? Probably, you have never asked yourself why it is a problem. Let us find out.

Sex is a problem because it would seem that in that act there is complete absence of the self. In that moment you are happy because there is the cessation of self-consciousness, of the 'me'; and desiring more of it—more of the abnegation of the self in which there is complete happiness, without the past or the future, demanding that complete happiness through full fusion, integration—naturally it becomes all-important. Isn't that so? Because it is something that gives me unadulterated joy, complete self-forgetfulness, I want more and more of it. Now, why do I want more of it? Because, everywhere else, I am in conflict, everywhere else, at all the different levels of existence, there is the strengthening of the self. Economically, socially, religiously, there is the constant thickening of self-consciousness, which is conflict.

After all, you are self-conscious only when there is conflict. Self-consciousness is in its very nature the result of conflict, so everywhere else we are in conflict. In all our relationships with property, with people, and with ideas there is conflict, pain, struggle, misery; but in this one act there is complete cessation of all that. Naturally you want more of it because it gives you happiness while all the rest leads you to misery, turmoil, conflict, confusion, antagonism, war, destruction; therefore, the sexual act becomes all-significant, all-important. So, the problem is not sex, surely, but how to be free from the self. You have tasted that state of being in which the self is not, if only for a few seconds, if only for a day, do what you will; and where the self is, there is conflict, there is misery, there is strife. So there is the constant longing for more of the self-free state. But the central problem is the conflict at different levels and how to negate the self. You are seeking happiness, that state in which the self, with all its conflicts, is not, which you find momentarily in that act. Or, you discipline yourself, you struggle, you control, you even destroy yourself through suppression—which means you are seeking to be free of conflict because with the cessation of conflict there is joy. If there can be freedom from conflict, there is happiness at all the different levels of existence.

— 6 —

What Is Wrong with Pleasure?

Now…why shouldn't one have pleasure? You see a beautiful sunset, a lovely tree, a river that has a wide, curving movement, or a beautiful face, and to look at it gives great pleasure, delight. What is wrong with that? It seems to me the confusion and the misery begin when that face, that river, that cloud, that mountain, becomes a memory, and this memory then demands a greater continuity of pleasure; we want such things repeated. We all know this. I have had a certain pleasure, or you have had a certain delight in something, and we want it repeated. Whether it be sexual, artistic, intellectual, or something not quite of this character, we want it repeated—and I think that is where pleasure begins to darken the mind and create values which are false, not actual.

What matters is to understand pleasure, not try to get rid of it—that is too stupid. Nobody can get rid of pleasure. But to understand the nature and the structure of pleasure, is essential; because if life is only pleasure, and if that is what one wants, then with pleasure go the misery, the confusion, the illusions, the false values which we create, and therefore there is no clarity.

— 7 —

When Pleasure Is not Fulfilled

Does one understand the pleasure of self-fulfillment, the pleasure of being somebody, of being recognized in the world as an author, as a painter, as a great man? Does one understand the pleasure of domination, the pleasure of money, the pleasure of taking the vow of poverty, the pleasure that one experiences in so many things? And does one see that when pleasure is not fulfilled, then begins the frustration, the bitterness, the cynicism? So one has to be aware of all this, not only physically, but psychologically; and then one begins to ask: What place has desire with regard to pleasure?

— 8 —

Is Pleasure Escape from Loneliness?

You know, there are two kinds of emptiness. There is the emptiness in which the mind looks at itself and says, "I am empty"; and there is the real emptiness. There is the emptiness I want to fill because I don't like that emptiness, that loneliness, that isolation, that sense of being completely cut off from everything. Each one of us must have had that feeling, either superficially, casually, or very intensely; and becoming aware of that feeling, one obviously escapes from it, one tries to cover it up with knowledge, or by means of relationship, the demand for a perfect union between man and woman, and all the rest of it. This is what actually takes place, isn't it? I am not inventing anything. If one has observed oneself, gone into oneself a little bit—not tremendously, that comes much later—one knows this to be a fact. So one begins to find out that where there is this sense of inexhaustible loneliness, this emptiness created by the mind's looking upon itself as being empty, there is also an urge, a tremendous drive to fulfill, to get something with which to cover it up.

So, consciously or unconsciously, one is aware of this state of—I don't like to use the word *emptiness* because emptiness is a beautiful word. A thing like a cup, or a room, is useful when it is empty; but if the cup is full, or the room is crowded with furniture, then it is useless. Most of us, being empty, fill ourselves with all kinds of noise, with pleasure and every form of escape.

— 9 —

Understanding Pleasure Is not to Deny It

Without understanding this pleasure, there is no ending of sorrow...

To understand pleasure is not to deny it, because pleasure is one of the basic demands of life, like enjoyment. When you see a beautiful tree, a lovely sunset, a nice smile on a face, light on a leaf, then you really enjoy it, there is great delight.

— 10 —

Do not Bring Thought into It

When you see something extraordinarily beautiful, full of life and beauty, you must never let thought come in, because the moment thought touches it, thought being old, it will pervert it into pleasure and, therefore, there arises the demand for pleasure and for more and more of pleasure; and when it is not given, there is conflict, there is fear. So, is it possible to look at a thing without thought?

CHAPTER SIX
Why Should We Change?

— I —

Change, and You Change the World

Now to understand the self, which alone can bring about a radical revolution, a regeneration, there must be the intention to understand its whole process. The process of the individual is not opposed to the world, to the mass, whatever that term may mean, because there is no mass apart from you—you are the mass.

— 2 —
Why Do We Want to Change?

First of all, why do we want to change *what is*, or bring about a transformation? Why? Because what we are dissatisfies us; it creates conflict, disturbance; and disliking that state, we want something better, something nobler, more idealistic. So, we desire transformation because there is pain, discomfort, conflict.

— 3 —
It Is Necessary

Because when you radically change, you are not changing because of society, you are not changing because you want to do good or you want to reach heaven or God or whatever it is. You are changing because it is necessary for itself. And if you love a thing for itself, then it brings about tremendous clarity, and it is this clarity that is going to bring about salvation to man—not doing good works and reforms.

— 4 —
Inward, not Outward, Change Transforms Society

There is no end to talking, to arguments, to explanations, but explanations, arguments, and talking do not lead to direct action because for that to take place, we need to change radically and fundamentally. That needs no argument. No convincing, no formula, no being influenced by another will make us change fundamentally, in the deep sense of that word. We do need to change, but not according to any particular idea or formula or concept, because when we have ideas about action, action ceases. Between action and idea there is a time interval, a lag, and in that time interval there is either resistance, conformity, or imitation of that idea or that formula and trying to put it into action. That's what most of us are doing all the time. We know we have to change, not only outwardly but deeply, psychologically.

The outward changes are many. They are forcing us to conform to a certain pattern of activity, but to meet the challenge of everyday life, there must be deep revolution. Most of us have an idea, a concept of what we should be or what we ought to be, but we never change fundamentally. Ideas, concepts of what one should be do not make us change at all. We only change when it is absolutely necessary, and we never see directly the necessity for change. When we do want to change, there is a great deal of conflict and resistance, and we waste a great deal of energy in resisting, in creating a barrier...

To bring about a good society, human beings have to change. You and I must find the energy, the impetus, the vitality to bring about this radical transformation of the mind, and that is not possible if we do not have enough energy. We need a great deal of energy to bring about a change within ourselves, but we waste our energy through conflict, through resistance, through conformity, through acceptance, through obedience. It is a waste of energy when we are trying to conform to a pattern. To conserve energy we must be aware of ourselves, how we dissipate energy. This is an age-long problem because most human beings are indolent. They would rather accept, obey, and follow. If we become aware of this indolence, this deep-rooted laziness, and try to quicken the mind and the heart, the intensity of it again becomes a conflict, which is also a waste of energy.

Our problem, one of the many that we have, is how to conserve this energy, the energy that is necessary for an explosion to take place in consciousness—an explosion that is not contrived, that is not put together by thought, but an explosion that occurs naturally when there is this energy that is not wasted...

We are talking about the necessity of gathering all energy to bring about a radical revolution in consciousness itself, because we must have a new mind; we must look at life totally differently.

CHAPTER SEVEN

What Is the Purpose of Life?

— I —

What Is the Purpose of Life?

The significance of life is living. Do we really live, is life worth
living when there is fear, when our whole life is trained in
imitation, in copying? In following authority, is there living? Are you living when you follow somebody, even if he
is the greatest saint or the greatest politician or the greatest
scholar?

If you observe your own ways, you will see that you do nothing but follow somebody or another. This process of following is what we call "living," and then at the end of it you say, "What is the significance of life?" To you, life has no significance now; the significance can come only when you put away all this authority. It is very difficult to put away authority.

What is freedom from authority? You can break a law. That is not the freedom from authority. But there is freedom in understanding the whole process, how the mind creates authority, how each one of us is confused and therefore wants to be assured that he is living the right kind of life. Because we want to be told what to do, we are exploited by gurus, spiritual as well as scientific. We do not know the significance of life as long as we are copying, imitating, following.

How can one know the significance of life when all that one is seeking is success? That is our life; we want success, we want to be completely secure inwardly and outwardly, we want somebody to tell us that we are doing right, that we are following the right path leading to salvation...All our life is following a tradition, the tradition of yesterday or of thousands of years, and we make every experience into an authority to help us to achieve a result. So, we do not know the significance of life. All that we know is fear—fear of what somebody says, fear of dying, fear of not getting what we want, fear of committing wrong, fear of doing good. Our minds are so confused, caught in theory, that we cannot describe what significance life has to us.

Life is something extraordinary. When the questioner asks, "What is the significance of life?" he wants a definition. All that he will know is the definition, mere words, and not the deeper significance, the extraordinary richness, the sensitivity to beauty, the immensity of living.

— 2 —

What Is Life?

So, in discussing what is the purpose of life, we have to find out what we mean by "life" and what we mean by "purpose"—not merely the dictionary meaning, but the significance we give to those words. Surely, life implies everyday action, everyday thought, everyday feeling, does it not? It implies the struggles, the pains, the anxieties, the deceptions, the worries, the routine of the office, of business, of bureaucracy, and so on. All of that is life, is it not? By life, we mean, not just one layer of consciousness, but the total process of existence which is our relationship to things, to people, to ideas. That is what we mean by life—not an abstract thing.

So, if that is what we mean by life, then has life a purpose? Or is it because we do not understand the ways of life—the everyday pain, anxiety, fear, ambition, greed—because we do not understand the daily activities of existence, that we want a purpose, remote or near, far away or close. We want a purpose so that we can guide our everyday life towards an end. That is obviously what we mean by purpose. But if I understand how to live, then the very living is in itself sufficient, is it not?...

After all, it is according to my prejudice, to my want, to my desire, to my predilection, that I decide what the purpose of life is to be. So, my desire creates the purpose. Surely, that is not the purpose of life. Which is more important—to find out the purpose of life, or to free the mind itself from its own conditioning and then inquire? And perhaps when the mind is free from is own conditioning, that very freedom itself is the purpose. Because, after all, it is only in freedom that one can discover any truth.

So, the first requisite is freedom, and not seeking the purpose of life.

— 3 —

What Is Life's Goal?

What is the significance of life? What is the purpose of life? Why do you ask such a question? You ask this question when, in you, there is chaos, and about you there is confusion, uncertainty. Belong uncertain, you want something to be certain. You want a certain purpose in life, a definite goal, because in yourself you are uncertain...

What is important is not what is the goal of life but to understand the confusion in which one is, the misery, the fears, and all the other things. We do not understand the confusion but only want to get rid of it. The real thing is here, not there. A man who is concerned does not ask what is the purpose of life. He is concerned with the clearing up of the confusion, of the sorrow in which he is caught.

— 4 —

To Understand, not Escape, Our Daily Tortures

To understand the full significance of living, we must understand the daily tortures of our complex life; we cannot escape from them. The society in which we live has to be understood by each one of us—not by some philosopher, not by some teacher, not by a guru—our way of living has to be transformed, completely changed. It think that is the most important thing we have to do, and nothing else.

— 5 —

Why Are We Alive?

Questioner: We live but we do not know why. To so many of us, life seems to have no meaning. Can you tell us the meaning and purpose of our living?

Krishnamurti: Now why do you ask this question? Why are you asking me to tell you the meaning of life, the purpose of life? What do we mean by life? Does life have a meaning, a purpose? Is not living in itself its own purpose, its own meaning? Why do we want more? Because we are so dissatisfied with our life, our life is so empty, so tawdry, so monotonous, doing the same thing over and over again, we want something more, something beyond that which we are doing. Since our everyday life is so empty, so dull, so meaningless, so boring, so intolerably stupid, we say life must have a fuller meaning and that is why you ask this question. Surely a man who is living richly, a man who sees things as they are and is content with what he has, is not confused; he is clear, therefore he does not ask what is the purpose of life. For him the very living is the beginning and the end. Our difficulty is that, since our life is empty, we want to find a purpose to life and strive for it. Such a purpose of life can only be mere intellection, without any reality; when the purpose of life is pursued by a stupid, dull mind, by an empty heart, that purpose will also be empty. Therefore our purpose is how to make our life rich, not with money and all the rest of it but inwardly rich—which is not something cryptic. When you say that the purpose of life is to be happy, the purpose of life is to find God, surely that desire to find God is an escape from life and your God is merely a thing that is known. You can only make your way towards an object which you know; if you build a staircase to the thing that you call God, surely that is not God. Reality can be understood only in living, not in escape. When you seek a purpose of life, you are really escaping and not understanding what life is. Life is relationship, life is action in relationship; when I do not understand relationship, or when relationship is confused, then I seek a fuller meaning. Why are our lives so empty? Why are we so lonely, frustrated? Because we have never looked into ourselves and understood ourselves. We never admit to ourselves that this life is all we know and that it should therefore be understood fully and completely. We prefer to run away from ourselves and that is why we seek the purpose of life away from relationship. If we begin to understand action, which is our relationship with people, with property, with beliefs and ideas, then we will find that relationship itself brings its own reward. You do not have to seek. It is like seeking love. Can you find love by seeking it? Love cannot be cultivated. You will find love only in relationship, not outside relationship, and it is because we have no love that we want a purpose of life. When there is love, which is its own eternity, then there is no search for God, because love is God.

It is because our minds are full of technicalities and superstitious mutterings that our lives are so empty and that is why we seek a purpose beyond ourselves. To find life's purpose we must go through the door of ourselves; consciously or unconsciously we avoid facing things as they are in themselves and so we want God to open for us a door which is beyond. This question about the purpose of life is put only by those who do not love. Love can be found only in action, which is relationship.

SECTION TWO

Self-Knowledge:
the Key to Freedom

CHAPTER ONE

Fear

— I —

Inner and Outer Fear

We are burdened with fear, not only outwardly, but inwardly. There is the outward fear of losing a job, of not having enough food to eat, of losing your position, of your boss behaving in an ugly manner. Inwardly also there is a great deal of fear—the fear of not being, of not becoming a success; the fear of death; the fear of loneliness; the fear of not being loved; the fear of utter boredom, and so on.

— 2 —

Fear Prevents Psychological Freedom

So our first problem, our really essential problem, is to be free from fear. You know what fear does? It darkens the mind. It makes the mind dull. From fear there is violence. From fear there is worship of something.

— 3 —

Physical Fear Is the Animal Response

Now, first there is the physical fear that is the animal response. Because we have inherited a great deal of the animal; a great part of our brain structure is the heritage of the animal. That is a scientific fact. It is not a theory, it is a fact. The animals are violent, so are human beings. The animals are greedy; they love to be flattered, they love to be petted; they like to find comfort; so do human beings. The animals are acquisitive, competitive; so are human beings. The animals live in groups; so do human beings like to function in groups. The animals have a social structure; so have human beings. We can go on much more in detail. But it is sufficient to see that there is a great deal in us which is still of the animal.

— 4 —

Can We Be Free of Both Animal and Cultural Conditioning

And is it possible for us not only to be free of the animal but also to go far beyond that and find out—not merely inquire verbally, but actually find out—whether the mind can go beyond the conditioning of a society, of a culture in which it is brought up? To discover, or to come upon, something which is totally of a different dimension, there must be freedom from fear.

— 5 —

Physical Fear that Protects the Body Is Intelligence; Psychological Fear Is Our Problem

Obviously self-protective reaction is not fear. We need food, clothes, and shelter—all of us, not only the rich, not only the high. Everybody needs them, and this cannot be solved by politicians. The politicians have divided the world into countries, like India, each with its separate sovereign government, with its separate army, and all this poisonous nonsense about nationalism. There is only one political problem, and that is to bring about human unity. And that cannot be brought about if you cling to your nationality, to your trivial divisions…When the house is burning, sir, you don't talk about the man who is bringing the water, you do not talk about the color of the hair of the man who set the house on fire, but you bring water. Nationalism has divided man, as religions have divided man, and this nationalist spirit and the religious beliefs have separated man, put man against man. And one can see why it has come into being. It is because we all like to live in a little puddle of our own.

And so, one has to be free from fear, and that is one of the most difficult things to do. Most of us are not aware that we are afraid, and we are not aware of what we are afraid. And when we know of what we are afraid, we do not know what to do. So we run away from what we are, which is fear; and what we run away to increases fear. And we have developed, unfortunately, a network of escapes.

— 6 —

The Origin of Fear

How does fear come about—fear of tomorrow, fear of losing a job, fear of death, fear of falling ill, fear of pain? Fear implies a process of thought about the future or about the past. I am afraid of tomorrow, of what might happen. I am afraid of death; it is at a distance still, but I am afraid of it. Now, what brings about fear? Fear always exists in relation to something. Otherwise there is no fear. So one is afraid of tomorrow or of what has been or what will be. What has brought fear? Isn't it thought?

— 7 —

Thought Is the Origin of Fear

So thought breeds fear. I think about my losing a job or I might lose a job, and thought creates the fear. So thought always projects itself in time, because thought is time. I think about the illness I have had and I do not like the pain, and I am frightened that the pain might return again. I have had an experience of pain; thinking about it and not wanting it create fear. Fear is very closely related to pleasure. Most of us are guided by pleasure. To us, like the animals, pleasure is of the highest importance, and pleasure is part of thought. By thinking about something that has given me pleasure, that pleasure is increased. Isn't it? Have you not noticed all this? You have had an experience of pleasure—of a beautiful sunset or of sex—and you think about it. The thinking about it increases pleasure, as thinking about what you have had as pain brings fear. So thought creates pleasure and fear. Doesn't it? So thought is responsible for the demand for, and the continuation of, pleasure; and thought is also responsible for engendering fear, bringing about fear. One sees this; this is an actual experimental fact.

Then one asks oneself, "Is it possible not to think about pleasure or pain? Is it possible to think only when thought is demanded, but not otherwise?" Sir, when you function in an office, when you are working at a job, thought is necessary; otherwise, you could not do anything. When you speak, when you write, when you talk, when you go to the office, thought is necessary. There, it must function precisely, impersonally. There, thought must not be guided by inclination, a tendency. There, thought is necessary. But is thought necessary in any other field of action?

Please follow this. For us thought is very important; that is the only instrument we have. Thought is the response of memory which has been accumulated through experience, through knowledge, through tradition; and memory is the result of time, inherited from the animal. And with this background we react. This reaction is thinking. Thought is essential at certain levels. But when thought projects itself as the future and the past psychologically, then thought creates fear as well as pleasure; and in this process the mind is made dull and, therefore, inaction is inevitable. Sir, fear, as we said, is brought about by thought—thinking about losing my job, thinking my wife might run away with somebody, thinking about death, thinking about what has been, and so on. Can thought stop thinking about the past psychologically, self-protectively, or about the future?

— 8 —

Attention without a Center

Therefore, one asks oneself, "Is it possible for thought to come to an end so that one lives completely, fully?" Have you ever noticed that when you attend completely, when you give your attention completely to anything, there is no observer and therefore no thinker, there is no center from which you are observing?

— 9 —
Attention Ends Fear

When you give such total and complete attention, there is no observer at all. And it is the observer that breeds fear because the observer is the center of thought; it is the 'me', the 'I', the self, the ego; the observer is the censor. When there is no thought, there is no observer. That state is not a blank state. That demands a great deal of inquiry—never accepting anything.

— 10 —
The Root of All Fear

Dependence on things, on people, or on ideas breeds fear; dependence arises from ignorance, from the lack of self-knowledge, from inward poverty; fear causes uncertainty of mind-heart, preventing communication and understanding. Through self-awareness we begin to discover and so comprehend the cause of fear, not only the superficial but the deep causal and accumulative fears. Fear is both inborn and acquired; it is related to the past, and to free thought-feeling from it, the past must be comprehended through the present. The past is ever wanting to give birth to the present which becomes the identifying memory of the 'me' and the 'mine', the 'I'. The self is the root of all fear.

CHAPTER TWO

Anger and Violence

— I —

Anger Can Be Self-Importance

Anger has that peculiar quality of isolation; like sorrow, it cuts one off, and for the time being, at least, all relationship comes to an end. Anger has the temporary strength and vitality of the isolated. There is a strange despair in anger; for isolation is despair. The anger of disappointment, of jealousy, of the urge to wound, gives a violent release whose pleasure is self-justification. We condemn others, and that very condemnation is a justification of ourselves. Without some kind of attitude, whether of self-righteousness or self-abasement, what are we? We use every means to bolster ourselves up; and anger, like hate, is one of the easiest ways. Simple anger, a sudden flare-up which is quickly forgotten, is one thing; but the anger that is deliberately built up, that has been brewed and that seeks to hurt and destroy, is quite another matter.

— 2 —

Physical and Psychological Roots of Anger

Simple anger may have some physiological cause which can be seen and remedied; but the anger that is the outcome of a psychological cause is much more subtle and difficult to deal with. Most of us do not mind being angry, we find an excuse for it. Why should we not be angry when there is ill-treatment of another or of ourselves? So we become righteously angry. We never just say we are angry, and stop there; we go into elaborate explanations of its cause. We never just say that we are jealous or bitter, but justify or explain it. We ask how there can be love without jealousy, or say that someone else's actions have made us bitter, and so on. It is the explanation, the verbalization, whether silent or spoken, that sustains anger, that gives it scope and depth. The explanation, silent or spoken, acts as a shield against the discovery of ourselves as we are. We want to be praised or flattered, we expect something; and when these things do not take place, we are disappointed, we become bitter or jealous. Then, violently or softly, we blame someone else; we say the other is responsible for our bitterness.

— 3 —

In Dependency Is Anger

You are of great significance because I depend upon you for my happiness, for my position or prestige. Through you, I fulfill, so you are important to me; I must guard you, I must possess you. Through you, I escape from myself; and when I am thrown back upon myself, being fearful of my own state, I become angry. Anger takes many forms: disappointment, resentment, bitterness, jealousy, and so on.

— 4 —

Stored Anger Is the Problem

The storing up of anger, which is resentment, requires the antidote of forgiveness; but the storing up of anger is far more significant than forgiveness. Forgiveness is unnecessary when there is no accumulation of anger. Forgiveness is essential if there is resentment; but to be free from flattery and from the sense of injury, without the hardness of indifference, makes for mercy, charity. Anger cannot be got rid of by the action of will, for will is part of violence. Will is the outcome of desire, the craving to be; and desire in its very nature is aggressive, dominant. To suppress anger by the exertion of will is to transfer anger to a different level, giving it a different name; but it is still part of violence. To be free from violence, which is not the cultivation of non-violence, there must be the understanding of desire.

— 5 —

Expectations Cause Pain and Anger

If you go into anger very deeply, not just brush it aside, then what is involved? Why is one angry? Because one is hurt, someone has said an unkind thing; and when someone says a flattering thing you are pleased. Why are you hurt? Self-importance, is it not? And why is there self-importance?

Because one has an idea, a symbol of oneself, an image of oneself, what one should be, what one is or what one should not be. Why does one create an image about oneself? Because one has never studied what one is, actually. We think we should be this or that, the ideal, the hero, the example. What awakens anger is that our ideal, the idea we have of ourselves, is attacked. And our idea about ourselves is our escape from the fact of what we are. But when you are observing the actual fact of what you are, no one can hurt you. Then, if one is a liar and is told that one is a liar it does not mean that one is hurt; it is a fact. But when you are pretending you are not a liar and are told that you are, then you get angry, violent. So we are always living in an ideational world, a world of myth, and never in the world of actuality. To observe *what is*, to see it, actually be familiar with it, there must be no judgment, no evaluation, no opinion, no fear.

— 6 —

Understanding Dissolves Anger

Surely that thing which you fight you become...If I am angry and you meet me with anger what is the result? More anger. You have become that which I am. If I am evil and you fight me with evil means then you also become evil, however righteous you may feel. If I am brutal and you use brutal methods to overcome me, then you become brutal like me. And this we have done for thousands of years. Surely there is a different approach than to meet hate by hate? If I use violent methods to quell anger in myself then I am using wrong means for a right end, and thereby the right end ceases to be. In this there is no understanding; there is no transcending anger. Anger is to be studied tolerantly and understood; it is not to be overcome through violent means. Anger may be the result of many causes, and without comprehending them there is no escape from anger.

We have created the enemy, the bandit, and becoming ourselves the enemy in no way brings about an end to enmity. We have to understand the cause of enmity and cease to feed it by our thought, feeling, and action. This is an arduous task demanding constant self-awareness and intelligent pliability, for what we are the society, the state, is. The enemy and the friend are the outcome of our thought and action. We are responsible for creating enmity and so it is more important to be aware of our own thought and action than to be concerned with the foe and the friend, for right thinking puts an end to division. Love transcends the friend and the enemy.

— 7 —

Individual Anger Is a Historical Process

We see the world of hate taking its harvest at the present. This world of hate has been created by our fathers and their forefathers and by us. Thus, ignorance stretches indefinitely into the past. It has not come into being by itself. It is the outcome of human ignorance, a historical process, isn't it? We as individuals have cooperated with our ancestors, who, with their forefathers, set going this process of hate, fear, greed, and so on. Now, as individuals, we partake of this world of hate so long as we, individually, indulge in it.

— 8 —

What You Are, the World Is

The world, then, is an extension of yourself. If you as an individual desire to destroy hate, then you as an individual must cease hating. To destroy hate, you must dissociate yourself from hate in all its gross and subtle forms, and so long as you are caught up in it you are part of that world of ignorance and fear. Then the world is an extension of yourself, yourself duplicated and multiplied. The world does not exist apart from the individual. It may exist as an idea, as a state, as a social organization, but to carry out that idea, to make that social or religious organization function, there must be the individual. His ignorance, his greed, and his fear maintain the structure of ignorance, greed, and hate. If the individual changes, can he affect the world, the world of hate, greed, and so on?...The world is an extension of yourself so long as you are thoughtless, caught up in ignorance, hate, greed, but when you are earnest, thoughtful, and aware, there is not only a dissociation from those ugly causes that create pain and sorrow, but also in that understanding there is a completeness, a wholeness.

— 9 —

The Causes of Anger and Violence

What are the causes of this terrible, destructive, brutal violence right through the world? I wonder if you have asked yourself this question, why? Or do you accept it as inevitable, as part of life?

Each one of us in his private life is also violent. We get angry; we do not like people to criticize us; we do not brook any interference with our particular lives; we are very defensive, and therefore aggressive, when we hold on to a particular belief of dogma, of when we worship our particular nationality, with the rag that is called the flag. So, individually, in our private, secret lives, we are aggressive, we are violent; and also outwardly, in our relationships with others. When we are ambitious, greedy, acquisitive, we are also outwardly, collectively aggressive, violent, and destructive.

I wonder why this is happening now, during this present period in history, and why it has always happened in the past? There have been so many wars, so many disruptive, destructive forces let loose on the world; why? What is the reason for it? Not that knowing the cause and the reason for it will ever free the mind from violence. But it is right to inquire into why human beings throughout the ages have been so violent, brutal, aggressive, cruel, destructive—destroying their own species. If you ask why, what do you think is the reason for it?—bearing in mind that explanations and conclusions do not in any way remove violence. We'll go into the question of freedom from violence, but first we must inquire why these violent reactions exist.

— 10 —
Inherited Biological Causes

I think one of the reasons is the instinct which we have inherited throughout the ages, which is derived from the animals. You have seen dogs fighting, or little bulls—the stronger fighting the weaker. The animals are aggressive and violent in nature. And as we human beings have evolved from them, we have also inherited this aggressive violence and hatred, which exists when we have territorial rights— rights over a piece of land—or sexual rights, as in the animal. So that is one of the causes.

— 11 —
Social and Environmental Causes

Then another cause is environment—the society in which we live, the culture in which we have been brought up, the education we have received. We are compelled by the society in which we live to be aggressive—each man fighting for himself, each man wanting a position, power, prestige.

His concern is about himself. Though he may also be concerned with the family, with the group, with the nation, and so on, essentially he is concerned with himself. He may work through the family, through the group, through the nation, but always he puts himself first. So the society in which we live is one of the contributory causes of this violence—that is the behavior which it imposes on us. In order to survive, it is said, you must be aggressive, you must fight. So environment has an extraordinary importance as a cause of violence, and this society in which we live is the product of all of us human beings; we ourselves have produced it.

— 12 —

Major Cause of Anger Is Psychological Demand for Security

But the major cause of violence, I think, is that each one of us is inwardly, psychologically, seeking security. In each one of us the urge for psychological security, that inward sense of being safe, projects the demand, the outward demand, for security. Inwardly each one of us wants to be secure, sure, certain. That is why we have all these marriage laws—in order that we may possess a woman, or a man, and so be secure in our relationship. If that relationship is attacked, we become violent, which is the psychological demand, the inward demand, to be certain of our relationship to everything. But there is no such thing as certainty, security, in any relationship. Inwardly, psychologically, we should like to be secure, but there is no such thing as permanent security. Your wife, your husband, may turn against you; your property may be taken away from you in a revolution.

— 13 —

Universal Outer and Inward Order

First, then, there must be order outwardly, and there cannot be order unless there is a universal language and a planning for the whole of mankind, which means the ending of all nationalities. Then, inwardly, there must be a freeing of the mind from all escapes so that it faces the fact of *what is*. Can I look at the fact of my being violent and not say, "I must not be violent," and not condemn it or justify it—just look at the fact of my being violent?

— 14 —

Revolt, Armies

There is obviously revolt within the pattern of society. Some revolts are respectable, others are not, but they are always within the field of society, within the limits of the social fence. And surely a society based on envy, on ambition, cruelty, war, must expect revolt within itself. After all, when you go to the cinema, the movies, you see a great deal of violence. There have been two enormous global wars, representing total violence. A nation which maintains an army must be destructive of its own citizens. Please listen to all this. No nation is peaceful as long as it has an army, whether it is a defensive or an offensive army. An army is both offensive and defensive; it does not bring about a peaceful state. The moment a culture establishes and maintains an army, it is destroying itself.

This is historically a fact.

— 15 —

Juvenile Delinquency

And on every side we are encouraged to be competitive, to be ambitious, to be successful. Competition, ambition, and success are the gods of a particularly prosperous society such as this, and what do you expect? You want juvenile delinquency to become respectable, that's all. You do not tackle the roots of the problem, which is to stop this whole process of war, of maintaining an army, of being ambitious, of encouraging competition. These things, which are rooted in our hearts, are the fences of society within which there is revolt going on all the time on the part of both the young and the old. The problem is not only that of juvenile delinquency, it involves our whole social structure, and there is no answer to it as long as you and I do not step totally out of society—society representing ambition, cruelty, the desire to succeed, to become somebody, to be on top. That whole process is essentially the egocentric pursuit of fulfillment, only it has been made respectable.

— 16 —
Do We Worship the Killer Competitor and thus Breed Anger?

How you worship a successful man! How you decorate a man who kills thousands! And there are all the divisions of belief, of dogma—the Christian and the Hindu, the Buddhist and the Muslim. These are the things that are bringing about conflict; and when you seek to deal with juvenile delinquency by merely keeping the children at home, or disciplining them, or putting them in the army, or having recourse to the various solutions offered by every psychologist and social reformer, you are surely dealing superficially with a fundamental question. But we are afraid to tackle fundamental questions because we would become unpopular, we would be termed communists or God knows what else, and labels seem to have extraordinary importance for most of us. Whether it is in Russia, in India, or here, the problem is essentially the same, and it is only when the mind understands this whole social structure that we shall find an entirely different approach to the problem, thereby perhaps establishing real peace, not this spurious peace of politicians.

CHAPTER THREE
Boredom and Interest

— I —

Are Causes Another Form of Escape?

Become a social worker or a political worker or a religious worker—is that it? Because you have nothing else to do, therefore you become a reformer! If you have nothing to do, if you are bored, why not be bored ? Why not *be* that? If you are in sorrow, *be* sorrowful. Don't try to find a way out of it, because your being bored has an immense significance, if you can understand it, live with it. If you say, "I am bored, therefore I will do something else", you are merely trying to escape from boredom, and, as most of our activities *are* escapes, you do much more harm socially and in every other way. The mischief is much greater when you escape than when you are what you are and remain with it. The difficulty is, how to remain with it and not run away; as most of our activities are a process of escape it is immensely difficult for you to stop escaping and face it. Therefore I am glad if you are really bored and I say, "Full stop, let's stay there, let's look at it. Why should you do anything?"

— 2 —

Why Are We Bored?

If you are bored, why are you bored ? What is the thing called boredom? Why is it that you are not interested in anything? There must be reasons and causes which have made you dull: suffering, escapes, beliefs, incessant activity, have made the mind dull, the heart unpliable. If you could find out why you are bored, why there is no interest, then surely you would solve the problem, wouldn't you? Then the awakened interest will function. If you are not interested in why you are bored, you cannot force yourself to be interested in an activity, merely to be doing something—like a squirrel going round in a cage. I know that this is the kind of activity most of us indulge in. But we can find out inwardly, psychologically, why we are in this state of utter boredom; we can see why most of us are in this state: we have exhausted ourselves emotionally and mentally; we have tried so many things, so many sensations, so many amusements. So many experiments, that we have become dull, weary. We join one group, do everything wanted of us and then leave it; we then go to something else, and try that. If we fail with one psychologist, we go to somebody else or to the priest; if we fail there, we go to another teacher, and so on; we always keep going. This process of constantly stretching and letting go *is* exhausting, isn't it? Like all sensations, it soon dulls the mind.

— 3 —

Boredom May Be Exhaustion

We have done that, we have gone from sensation to sensation, from excitement to excitement, till we come to a point when we are really exhausted. Now, realizing that, don't proceed any further; take a rest. Be quiet. Let the mind gather strength by itself; don't force it. As the soil renews itself during the winter time, so, when the mind is allowed to be quiet, it renews itself. But it is very difficult to allow the mind to be quiet, to let it lie fallow after all this, for the mind wants to be doing something all the time. When you come to that point where you are really allowing yourself to be as you are—bored, ugly, hideous, or whatever it is—then there is a possibility of dealing with it.

What happens when you accept something, when you accept what you are? When you accept that you are what you are, where is the problem? There is a problem only when we do not accept a thing as it is and wish to transform it—which does not mean that I am advocating contentment; on the contrary. If we accept what we are, then we see that the thing which we dreaded, the thing which we called boredom, the thing which we called despair, the thing which we called fear, has undergone a complete change. There is a complete transformation of the thing of which we were afraid.

— 4 —

Is Our Interest in Something Based Only in Reward?

What do you mean by interest? Why is there this change from interest to boredom? What does interest mean? You are interested in that which pleases you, gratifies you, are you not? Is not interest a process of acquisitiveness? You would not be interested in anything if you did not get something out of it, would you?' There is sustained interest as long as you are acquiring; acquisition is interest, is it not? You have tried to gain satisfaction from everything you have come in contact with; and when you have thoroughly used it, naturally you get bored with it. Every acquisition is a form of boredom, weariness. We want a change of toys; as soon as we lose interest in one, we turn to another, and there is always a new toy to turn to. We turn to something in order to acquire; there is acquisition in pleasure, in knowledge, in fame, in power, in efficiency, in having a family, and so on. When there is nothing further to acquire in one religion, in one savior, we lose interest and turn to another. Some go to sleep in an organization and never wake up, and those who do wake up put themselves to sleep again by joining another. This acquisitive movement is called expansion of thought, progress.

"Is interest always acquisition?"

Actually, are you interested in anything which doesn't give you something, whether it be a play, a game, a conversation, a book, or a person? If a painting doesn't give you something, you pass it by; if a person doesn't stimulate or disturb you in some way, if there is no pleasure or pain in a particular relationship, you lose interest, you get bored. Haven't you noticed this?

"Yes, but I have never before looked at it in this way."

You wouldn't have come here if you didn't want something. You want to be free of boredom. As I cannot give you that freedom, you will get bored again; but if we can together understand the process of acquisition, of interest, of boredom, then perhaps there will be freedom. Freedom cannot be acquired. If you acquire it, you will soon be bored with it. Does not acquisition dull the mind? Acquisition, positive or negative, is a burden. As soon as you acquire, you lose interest. In trying to possess, you are alert, interested; but possession is boredom. You may want to possess more, but the pursuit of more is only a movement towards boredom. You try various forms of acquisition, and as long as there is the effort to acquire, there is interest; but there is always an end to acquisition, and so there is always boredom. Isn't this what has been happening?

— 5 —

Renewal Lies between Thoughts

The difficulty is for the mind to be still; for the mind is always worried, it is always after something, acquiring or denying, searching and finding. The mind is never still, it is in continuous movement. The past, overshadowing the present, makes its own future. It is a movement in time, and there is hardly ever an interval between thoughts. One thought follows another without pause; the mind is ever making itself sharp and so wearing itself out. If a pencil is being sharpened all the time, soon there will be nothing left of it; similarly, the mind uses itself constantly and is exhausted. The mind is always afraid of coming to an end. But, living is ending from day to day; it is the dying to all acquisition, to memories, to experiences, to the past.

CHAPTER FOUR
Self-Pity; Sorrow; Suffering

— I —
What Is Sorrow?

Man has tried to overcome sorrow in so many ways—
through worship, through escape, through drink, through
entertainment—but it is always there. Sorrow has to be understood as you would understand any other thing. Do not
deny it, do not suppress it, do not try to overcome it; but
understand it, look at what it is. What is sorrow? Do you
know what sorrow is?

— 2 —

Sorrow Is Loneliness

Sorrow is when you lose somebody whom you think you love; sorrow is when you cannot fulfill totally, completely; sorrow is when you are denied opportunity, capacity; sorrow is when you want to fulfill and there is no way to fulfill; sorrow is when you are confronted by your own utter emptiness, loneliness; and sorrow is burdened with self-pity. Do you know what "self-pity" is?

— 3 —

Self-Pity Is a Factor of Sorrow

Self-pity is when you complain about yourself unconsciously or consciously, when you are pitying yourself, when you say, "I can't do anything against the environment in which I am, placed as I am;" when you call yourself a pest, bemoaning your own lot. And so there is sorrow.

To understand sorrow, first, one has to be aware of this self-pity. It is one of the factors of sorrow. When someone dies, you are left and you become aware of how lonely you are. Or, if someone dies, you are left without any money, you are insecure. You have lived on others and you begin to complain, you begin to have self-pity. That is a fact, like the fact that you are lonely; that is *what is*. Look at self-pity, do not try to overcome it, do not deny it or say, "What am I to do with it?" The fact is: There is self-pity. The fact is: You are lonely. Can you look at it without any comparison of how extraordinarily secure you were yesterday, when you had that money or that person or that capacity—whatever it is? Just look at it; then you will see that self-pity has no place at all.

— 4 —

The Sorrow of Loneliness

One of the factors of sorrow is the extraordinary loneliness of man. You may have companions, you may have gods, you may have a great deal of knowledge, you may be extraordinarily active socially...and still this loneliness remains. Therefore, man seeks to find significance in life and invents a significance, a meaning. But the loneliness still remains. So can you look at it without any comparison, just see it as it is, without trying to run away from it, without trying to cover it up, or to escape from it? Then you will see that loneliness becomes something entirely different.

— 5 —

Loneliness Is Sorrow: Standing Alone Is Freedom

Man must be alone. We are not alone. We are the result of a thousand influences, a thousand conditionings, psychological inheritances, propaganda, culture. We are not alone, and therefore we are secondhand human beings. When one is alone, totally alone, neither belonging to any family, though one may have a family, nor belonging to any nation, to any culture, to any particular commitment, there is the sense of being an outsider—outsider to every form of thought, action, family, nation. And it is only the one who is completely alone who is innocent. It is this innocency that frees the mind from sorrow.

— 6 —

Are Those Tears for Yourself, or the One Who Is Dead?

Are you experiencing sorrow as strongly and urgently as you would a toothache? When you have a toothache, you act; you go to the dentist. But when there is sorrow you run away from it through explanation, belief, drink, and so on. You act, but your action is not the action that frees the mind from sorrow, is it?

"I don't know what to do, and that's why I'm here."

Before you can know what to do, must you not find out what sorrow actually is? Haven't you merely formed an idea, a judgment, of what sorrow is? Surely, the running away, the evaluation, the fear, prevents you from experiencing it directly. When you are suffering from a toothache, you don't form ideas and opinions about it; you just have it and act. But here there is no action, immediate or remote, because you are really not suffering. To suffer and to understand suffering, you must look at it, you must not run away.

"My father is gone beyond recall, and so I suffer. What must I do to go beyond the reaches of suffering?"

We suffer because we do not see the truth of suffering. The fact and our ideation about the fact are entirely distinct, leading in two different directions. If one may ask, are you concerned with the fact, the actuality, or merely with the idea of suffering?

"You are not answering my question, sir," he insisted. "What am I to do?"

— 7 —

Freedom from the Poison of Self-Pity

Do you want to escape from suffering, or to be free from it? If you merely want to escape, then a pill, a belief, an explanation, an amusement may 'help', with the inevitable consequences of dependence, fear, and so on. But if you wish to be free from sorrow, you must stop running away and be aware of it without judgment, without choice; you must observe it, learn about it, know all the intimate intricacies of it. Then you will not be frightened of it, and there will no longer be the poison of self-pity. With the understanding of sorrow there is freedom from it. To understand sorrow there must be the actual experiencing of it, and not the verbal fiction of sorrow.

— 8 —

How Then Do I Live My Daily Life?

"May I ask just one question?" put in one of the others. "In what manner should one live one's daily life?"

As though one were living for that single day, for that single hour.

"How?"

If you had only one hour to live, what would you do?

"I really don't know," he replied anxiously.

Would you not arrange what is necessary outwardly, your affairs, your will, and so on? Would you not call your family and friends together and ask their forgiveness for the harm that you might have done to them, and forgive them for whatever harm they might have done to you? Would you not die completely to the things of the mind, to desires and to the world? And if it can be done for an hour, then it can also be done for the days and years that may remain.

"Is such a thing really possible, sir?"

Try it and you will find out.

— 9 —
Understanding Suffering

What is the good of my asking if there is happiness when I am suffering? Can I understand suffering? That is my problem, not how to be happy. I am happy when I am not suffering, but the moment I am conscious of it, it is not happiness...So I must understand what is suffering. Can I understand what is suffering when a part of my mind is running away seeking happiness, seeking a way out of this misery? So must I not, if I am to understand suffering, be completely one with it, not reject it, not justify it, not condemn it, not compare it, but completely be with it and understand it?

The truth of what is happiness will come if I know how to listen. I must know how to listen to suffering; if I can listen to suffering I can listen to happiness, because that is what I am.

— 10 —
Suffering Is Suffering: Everyone's Brain and Pain Are the Same

Is your suffering as an individual different from my suffering, or from the suffering of a man in Asia, in America, or in Russia? The circumstances, the incidents may vary, but in essence another man's suffering is the same as mine and yours, isn't it? Suffering is suffering, surely, not yours or mine. Pleasure is not your pleasure, or my pleasure—it is pleasure. When you are hungry, it is not your hunger only, it is the hunger of the whole of Asia too. When you are driven by ambition, when you are ruthless, it is the same ruthlessness that drives the politician, the man in power, whether he is in Asia, in America, or in Russia.

You see, that is what we object to. We don't see that we are all one humanity, caught in different spheres of life, in different areas. When you love somebody, it is not your love. If it is, it becomes tyrannical, possessive, jealous, anxious, brutal. Similarly, suffering is suffering; it is not yours or mine. I am not just making it impersonal, I am not making it something abstract. When one suffers, one suffers. When a man has no food, no clothing, no shelter, he is suffering, whether he lives in Asia, or in the West. The people who are now being killed or wounded—the Vietnamese and the Americans—are suffering. To under- stand this suffering—which is neither yours nor mine, which is not impersonal or abstract, but actual and which we all have—requires a great deal of penetration, insight. And the ending of this suffering will naturally bring about peace, not only within, but outside.

CHAPTER FIVE

Jealousy; Possessiveness; Envy

— 1 —

To Think We Own a Human Being Makes Us Feel Important

Jealousy is one of the ways of holding the man or the woman, is it not? The more we are jealous, the greater the feeling of possession. To possess something makes us happy; to call something, even a dog, exclusively our own makes us feel warm and comfortable. To be exclusive in our possession gives us assurance and certainty to ourselves. To own something makes us important; it is this importance we cling to. To think that we own, not a pencil or a house, but a human being, makes us feel strong and strangely content. Envy is not because of the other, but because of the worth, the importance of ourselves.

"But I am not important, I am nobody; my husband is all that I have. Even my children don't count."

We all have only one thing to which we cling, though it takes different forms. You cling to your husband, others to their children, and yet others to some belief; but the intention is the same. Without the object to which we cling we feel so hopelessly lost, do we not? We are afraid to feel all alone. This fear is jealousy, hate, pain. There is not much difference between envy and hate.

— 2 —

Jealousy Is Not Love

"But we love each other."

Then how can you be jealous? We do not love, and that is the unfortunate part of it. You are using your husband, as he is using you, to be happy, to have a companion, not to feel alone; you may not possess much, but at least you have someone to be with. This mutual need and use we call love.

"But this is dreadful."

It is not dreadful, only we never look at it. We call it dreadful, give it a name and quickly look away—which is what you are doing.

"I know, but I don't want to look. I want to carry on as I am, even though it means being jealous, because I cannot see anything else in life."

If you saw something else you would no longer be jealous of your husband, would you? But you would cling to the other thing as now you are clinging to your husband, so you would be jealous of that too. You want to find a substitute for your husband, and not freedom from jealousy. We are all like that: before we give up one thing, we want to be very sure of another. When you are completely uncertain, then only is there no place for envy. There is envy when there is certainty, when you feel that you have something. Exclusiveness is this feeling of certainty; to own is to be envious. Ownership breeds hatred. We really hate what we possess, which is shown in jealousy. Where there is possession there can never be love; to possess is to destroy love.

— 3 —

Attachment to Reputation, Things, a Person, Causes Pain

The present culture is based on envy, on acquisitiveness... Success is pursued in different ways, success as an artist, as a businessman, as a religious aspirant. All this is a form of envy, but it is only when envy becomes distressing, painful, that one attempts to get rid of it. As long as it is compensating and pleasurable, envy is an accepted part of one's nature. We don't see that in this very pleasure there is pain. Attachment does give pleasure, but it also breeds jealousy and pain, and it is not love. In this area of activity one lives, suffers, and dies. It is only when the pain of this self-enclosing action becomes unbearable that one struggles to break through it.

"I think I vaguely grasp all this, but what am I to do?"

Before considering what to do, let us see what the problem is. What is the problem?

"I am tortured by jealousy and I want to be free from it."

You want to be free from the pain of it; but don't you want to hold on to the peculiar pleasure that comes with possession and attachment?

"Of course I do. You don't expect me to renounce all my possession, do you?"

We are not concerned with renunciation but with the desire to possess. We want to possess people as well as things, we cling to beliefs as well as hopes. Why is there this desire to own things and people, this burning attachment?

"I don't know, I have never thought about it. It seems natural to be envious, but it has become a poison, a violently disturbing factor in my life."

We do need certain things, food, clothing, shelter, and so on, but they are used for psychological satisfaction, which gives rise to many other problems. In the same way, psychological dependence on people breeds anxiety, jealousy and fear.

"I suppose in that sense I do depend on certain people. They are a compulsive necessity to me, and without them I would be totally lost. If I did not have my husband and children I think I would go slowly mad, or I would attach my-self to somebody else. But I don't see what is wrong with attachment."

We are not saying it is right or wrong but are considering its cause and effect, are we not? We are not condemning or justifying dependence. But why is one psychologically dependent on another?

"I know I am dependent, but I haven't really thought about it. I took it for granted that everyone is dependent on another."

— 4 —

Physical Dependence Is not Psychological Dependence

Of course we are physically dependent on each other and always will be, which is natural and inevitable. But as long as we do not understand our *psychological* dependence on another don't you think the pain of jealousy will continue? So why is there this psychological need of another?

"I need my family because I love them. If I didn't love them I wouldn't care…"

You want to keep the pleasure of attachment and let the pain of it go. Is this possible?

"Why not?"

Attachment implies fear, does it not? You are afraid of what you are, or of what you will be if the other leaves you or dies, and you are attached because of this fear. As long as you are occupied with the pleasure of attachment, fear is hidden, locked away, but unfortunately it is always there; and till you are free from this fear, the tortures of jealousy will go on.

— 5 —

The Top of the Heap

Do you know what life is? It extends from the moment you are born to the moment you die, and perhaps beyond. Life is a vast, complex whole; it's like a house in which everything is happening at once. You love and you hate; you are greedy, envious, and at the same time you feel you shouldn't be. You are ambitious, and there is either frustration or success, following in the wake of anxiety, fear and ruthlessness; and sooner or later there comes a feeling of the futility of it all. Then there are the horrors and brutality of war, and peace through terror; there is nationalism, sovereignty, which supports war; there is death at the end of life's road, or anywhere along it. There is the search for God, with its conflicting beliefs and the quarrels between organized religions. There is the struggle to get and keep a job; there are marriage, children, illness, and the dominance of society and the State. Life is all this, and much more; and you are thrown into this mess. Generally you sink into it, miserable and lost; and if you survive by climbing to the top of the heap, you are still part of the mess. This is what we call life: everlasting struggle and sorrow, with a little joy occasionally thrown in. Who is going to teach you about all this? Or rather, how are you going to learn about it? Even if you have capacity and talent, you are bounded by ambition, by the desire for fame, with its frustrations and sorrows. All this is life, isn't it? And to go beyond all this is also life.

— 6 —

The Vicious Frame

That is just it. Everyone says that he must make his way through life; each one is out for himself, whether in the name of business, religion or the country. You want to become famous, and so does your neighbor, and so does *his* neighbor: and so it is with everyone, from the highest to the lowest in the lane. Thus we build a society based on ambition, envy, and acquisitiveness, in which each man is the enemy of another; and you are 'educated' to conform to this disintegrating society, to fit into its vicious frame.

"But what are we to do?" asked the second one. "It seems to me that we must conform to society or be destroyed. Is there any way out of it, sir?"

At present you are so-called educated to fit into this society; your capacities are developed to enable you to make a living within the pattern. Your parents your educators your government, are all concerned with your efficiency and financial security, are they not?

Yes, they want you to be 'good citizens', which means being respectably ambitious, everlastingly acquisitive, and indulging in that socially accepted ruthlessness which is called competition, so that you and they may be secure. This is what constitutes being a so-called good citizen; but is it good, or something very evil?...Love implies—doesn't it?—that those who are loved be left wholly free to grow in their fullness, to be something greater than mere social machines. Love does not compel, either openly or through the subtle threat of duties and responsibilities.

— 7 —
Is Duty Love?

What parents call duty is not love, it's a form of compulsion; and society will support the parents, for what they are doing is very respectable...They consider it a necessity for him to conform to society, to be respectable and secure. This is called love. But is it love? Or is it fear, covered over by the word 'love?'

— 8 —
Ambition Is Envy, Division, War

The older people say that you, the coming generation, must create a different world, but they don't mean it at all. On the contrary, with great thought and care they set about 'educating' you to conform to the old pattern, with some modification. Though they may talk very differently, teachers and parents, supported by the government and society in general, see to it that you are trained to conform to tradition, to accept ambition and envy as the natural way of life. They are not at all concerned with a new way of life, and that is why the educator himself is not being rightly educated. The older generation has brought about this world of war, this world of antagonism and division between man and man; and the newer generation is following sedulously in its footsteps.

"But we want to be rightly educated, sir. What shall we do?"

First of all, see very clearly one simple fact: that neither the government, nor your present teachers, nor your parents, care to educate you rightly; if they did, the world would be entirely different, and there would be no wars. So if you want to be rightly educated, you have to set about it yourself; and when you are grown up, you will then see to it that your own children are rightly educated.

"But how can we rightly educate ourselves? We need someone to teach us." You have teachers to instruct you in mathematics, in literature, and so on; but education is something deeper and wider than the mere gathering of information. Education is the cultivation of the mind so that action is not self-centered; it is learning throughout life to break down the walls which the mind builds in order to be secure, and from which arises fear with all its complexities. To be rightly educated, you have to study hard and not be lazy. Be good at games, not to beat another, but to amuse yourself. Eat the right food, and keep physically fit. Let the mind be alert and capable of dealing with the problems of life, not as a Hindu, a Communist, or a Christian, but as a human being. To be rightly educated, you have to understand yourself; you have to keep on learning about yourself. When you stop learning, life becomes ugly and sorrowful. Without goodness and love, you are not rightly educated.

CHAPTER SIX

Desire and Longing

— I —

The Pain in Desire Is Fear of Frustration

For most of us, desire is quite a problem—the desire for property, for position, for power, for comfort, for immortality, for continuity, the desire to be loved, to have something permanent, satisfying, lasting, something which is beyond time. Now, what is desire? What is this thing that is urging, compelling us?—which doesn't mean that we should be satisfied with what we have or with what we are, which is merely the opposite of what we want. We are trying to see what desire is, and if we can go into it tentatively, hesitantly, I think we will bring about a transformation which is not a mere substitution of one object of desire for another object of desire. But this is generally what we mean by "change," is it not? Being dissatisfied with one particular object of desire, we find a substitute for it. We are everlastingly moving from one object of desire to another which we consider to be higher, nobler, more refined, but however refined, desire is still desire, and in this movement of desire there is endless struggle, the conflict of the opposites.

So, is it not important to find out what is desire and whether it can be transformed?...And can I dissolve that center of desire—not one particular desire, one particular appetite or craving, but the whole structure of desire, of longing, hoping, in which there is always the fear of frustration? The more I am frustrated, the more strength I give to the 'me'. As long as there is hoping, longing, there is always the background of fear, which again strengthens that center...

Beyond the physical needs, any form of desire—for greatness, for truth, for virtue—becomes a psychological process by which the mind builds the idea of the 'me' and strengthens itself at the center.

— 2 —
Follow the Movement of Desire

Desire means the urge to fulfill appetites of various kinds that demands action—the longing for sex, or to become a great man, the desire to possess a car...

So, what is desire? You see a beautiful house or a nice car or a man in power, position; and you wish you had that house, you were that man in position, or you were riding amid applause. How does that desire arise? First, there is the visual perception—the seeing of the house. The 'you' comes much later. The seeing of the house, that is visual attraction, the attraction of a line, the beauty of a car, the color, and then that perception.

Please follow this. You are doing it, not I. I am giving words, explaining; but you are doing. We are sharing the thing together. You are not merely listening to what the speaker is saying; therefore, you are observing your own movement of thought as desire. There is no division between thought and seeing; they are one movement. Between thought and desire, there is no separate thing—which we will go into presently.

— 3 —
The Rise of Desire

So there is the seeing, the perceiving, which creates sensation; then there is the touching; and then the desire—the desire to possess—to give to that sensation continuity. This is very simple. I see a beautiful woman or a man. Then there is the pleasure of seeing, and the pleasure demands continuity. So I think; there is thought born out of it. And the more thought thinks about that pleasure, there is continuity of that pleasure, or of that pain. Then, where there is that continuity, the 'I' comes in—I want, I don't want. This is what we all do, all day, sleeping or waking.

So, one sees how desire arises. Perception, contact, sensation; then giving to that sensation continuity, and that continuity to sensation is desire. There is nothing mysterious about desire. Now the desire becomes very complicated when there is a contradiction, not in the desire itself, but in the object through which it is going to fulfill. Right? I want to be a very rich man—that is, my desire says that I must be very rich because I see people with property, a car and all the rest of it. Desire says, "I must have, I must fulfill."

— 4 —

Desire Must Be Understood, not Throttled

Desire wants to fulfill itself in every direction; the objects of fulfillment are very attractive, but each object contradicts the other.

So we live, conforming, battling fulfilling, and being frustrated. That is our life. And to find God, the so-called religious people, the saints, the popes, the monks, the nuns, the social-service people, the so-called religious people say, "You must suppress; you must sublimate; you must identify yourself with God so that desire disappears; when you see a woman, turn your back on her; don't be sensitive to anything, to life; don't hear music, don't see a tree; above all, don't see a woman!" And so that is the life of the mediocre man who is a slave to society!

Without understanding—understanding, not suppressing—desire, man will never be free of conformity or fear. You know what happens when you suppress something? Your heart is dull! Have you seen the sannyasis, the monks, the nuns, the people who escape from life? How frigid, how hard, virtuous, saintly they are, living in tight discipline! They will talk everlastingly about love, and inwardly they are boiling; their desires never fulfilled or never understood; they are dead beings in a cloak of virtue!

What we are saying is something entirely different…one has to find out, learn, about desire—learn, not what to do about it, not how to throttle it.

— 5 —

With Understanding, Desire Happens but Does not Take Root

Desire creates contradiction, and the mind that is at all alert does not like to live in contradiction; therefore, it tries to get rid of desire. But if the mind can understand desire without trying to brush it away, without saying, "This is a better desire and that is a worse one, I am going to keep this and discard the other;" if it can be aware of the whole field of desire without rejecting, without choosing, without condemning, then you will see that the mind becomes very quiet; desires come, but they no longer have impact; they are no longer of great significance; they do not take root in the mind and create problems. The mind reacts; otherwise it would not be alive, but the reaction is superficial and does not take root. That is why it is important to understand this whole process of desire in which most of us are caught.

— 6 —

Can We Have Desire without Having to Act on It?

But for most of us desire means self-indulgence, self-expression: I desire that, and I must have it. Whether it is a beautiful person, or a house, or an idea, I must have it. Why? Why does the "must" come into being? Why does desire say, "I must have that"—which brings about the agony, the drive, the urge, the demands of a compulsive existence? It is fairly simple, fairly clear, why there is this insistence on self-expression, which is a form of desire. In self-expression, in being somebody, there is great delight because you are recognized. People say, "By Jove, do you know who he is?"—and all the rest of that nonsense. You may say that it isn't just desire, it isn't just pleasure, because there is something behind desire which is much stronger still. But you cannot come to that without understanding pleasure and desire. The active process of desire and pleasure is what we call action. I want something, and I work, work, work to get it. I want to be famous as a writer, painter, and I do everything I can think of to become famous. Generally I fall by the wayside and never get recognized by the world, so I am frustrated, I go through agony; and then I become cynical, or I take on the pretense of humility, and all the rest of that nonsense begins.

— 7 —

Why Are We so Full of Longing?

So we are asking ourselves: Why is there this insistence on desire being fulfilled? If you want a coat, a suit, a shirt, a tie, a pair of shoes, you get it—that is one thing. But behind this persistent drive to fulfill oneself, surely, there is the sense of complete inadequacy, loneliness. I can't live by myself, I can't be alone, because in myself I am insufficient. You know more than I do, you are more beautiful, more intellectual, more clever, you are more this and more that, and I want to be all those things and more. Why? I do not know whether you have ever asked yourself this question. If you have, and if for you it is not just a clever theoretical question, then you will find the answer...

I want to know why one craves many things, or one thing. One wants to be happy, to find God, to be rich, to be famous, to be complete, or to be liberated, whatever that may mean—you know all the things, a craving for which one builds up. One wants to have a perfect marriage, a perfect relationship with God, and so on. Why? First of all, it indicates how shallow the mind is, doesn't it? And doesn't it also indicate our own sense of loneliness, emptiness?

— 8 —

Desire Itself Is not the Problem: Only What We Do about It

Let us go on to consider desire. We know, do we not, the desire which contradicts itself, which is tortured, pulling in different directions; the pain, the turmoil, the anxiety of desire, and the disciplining, the controlling. And in the everlasting battle with it we twist it out of all shape and recognition; but it is there, constantly watching, waiting, pushing. Do what you will, sublimate it, escape from it, deny it or accept it, give it full rein—it is always there. And we know how the religious teachers and others have said that we should be desireless, cultivate detachment, be free from desire—which is really absurd, because desire has to be understood, not destroyed. If you destroy desire, you may destroy life itself. If you pervert desire, shape it, control it, dominate it, suppress it, you may be destroying something extraordinarily beautiful.

CHAPTER SEVEN

Self-Esteem: Success and Failure

— I —

Self-Esteem

We all place ourselves at various levels, and we are constantly falling from these heights. It is the falls we are ashamed of. Self-esteem is the cause of our shame, of our fall. It is this self-esteem that must be understood, and not the fall. If there is no pedestal on which you have put yourself, how can there be any fall?

— 2 —

You Are What You Are

Why have you put yourself on a pedestal called self-esteem, human dignity, the ideal, and so on? If you can understand this, then there will be no shame of the past; it will have completely gone. You will be what you are without the pedestal. If the pedestal is not there, the height that makes you look down or look up, then you *are* what you have always avoided. It is this avoidance of what *is*, of what you are, that brings about confusion and antagonism, shame and resentment. You do not have to tell me or another what you are, but be aware of what you are, whatever it is, pleasant or unpleasant: live with it without justifying or resisting it. Live with it without naming it; for the very term is a condemnation or identification. Live with it without fear, for fear prevents communion.

— 3 —

Ambition Clouds Clarity

Questioner: Sir, what is the function of thought in everyday life?

Krishnamurti: The function of thought is to be reasonable, to think clearly, objectively, efficiently, precisely; and you cannot think precisely, clearly, efficiently if you are tethered to your own personal vanity, to your own success, to you own fulfillment.

— 4 —

Ambition Is Fear

What has ambition done in the world? So few have ever thought about it. When somebody is struggling to be on the top of somebody else, when everybody is trying to achieve, to gain, have you ever found out what is in their hearts? If you will look at your own heart and see when you are ambitious, when you are struggling to be somebody, spiritually or in the world, you find that there is the worm of fear inside it. The ambitious man is the most frightened man because he is afraid to be what he is, because he says, "If I am what I am, I shall be nobody. Therefore, I must be somebody, I must become the engineer, the engine driver, the magistrate, the judge, the minister."

— 5 —

Is Interest the Same as Ambition?

Questioner: If somebody has an ambition to be an engineer, does it not mean that he is interested in it?

Krishnamurti: Would you say being interested in something is ambition? We can give to that word *ambition* any meaning. Ambition, as we generally know it, is the outcome of fear. Now, if I am interested as a boy in being an engineer because I love it, because I want to build beautiful houses, because I want to have the best irrigation in the world, because I want to build the best roads, it means I love the thing; therefore, that is not ambition. In that, there is no fear.

So, ambition and interest are two different things, are they not? I am interested in painting, I love it, I do not want to compete with the best painter or the most famous painter, I just love painting. You may be better at painting, but I do not compare myself with you. I love what I am doing when I paint; that in itself is sufficient for me.

— 6 —

Do What You Love

So, is it not very important when you are young, when you are in a place like this, to help you to awaken your own intelligence so that you will naturally find your vocation? Then, if you find it and if it is a true thing, then you will love it right through life. In that, there will be no ambition, no competition, no struggle, no fighting each other for position, for prestige; and perhaps then you will be able to create a new world. Then, in that world, all the ugly things of the old generation will not exist—their wars, their mischief, their separative gods, their rituals which mean absolutely noth-ing, their government, their violence. In a place of this kind, the responsibility of the teacher and of you is very great be-cause you can create a new world, a new culture, a new way of life.

— 7 —

If You Love Flowers, Be a Gardener

So, what happens in the world is that everybody is fighting somebody. One man is lesser than another man. There is no love, there is no consideration, there is no thought. Each man wants to become somebody. A member of parliament wants to become the leader of the parliament, to become the prime minister, and so on and on and on. There is perpetual fight-ing, and our society is one constant struggle of one man against another, and this struggle is called the ambition to be something. Old people encourage you to do that. You must be ambitious, you must be something, you must marry a rich man or a rich woman, you must have the right kind of friends. So, the older generation, those who are frightened, those who are ugly in their hearts, try to make you like them, and you also want to be like them because you see the glam-our of it all. When the governor comes, everybody bows...

That is why it is very important that you should find the right vocation. You know what "vocation" means? Some-thing which you will love to do, which is natural. After all, that is the function of education, of a school of this kind, to help you grow independently so that you are not ambitious but can find your true vocation. The ambitious man has never found his true vocation...

That is not ambition, to do something marvelously, completely, truly according to what you think; that is not ambition; in that there is no fear.

— 8 —

Comparison Breeds Competition, Ambition

We are always comparing ourselves with somebody else. If I am dull, I want to be more clever. If I am shallow, I want to be deep. If I am ignorant, I want to be more clever, more knowledgeable. I am always comparing myself, measuring myself against others—a better car, better food, a better home, a better way of thinking. Comparison breeds conflict. And do you understand through comparison? When you compare two pictures, two pieces of music, two sunsets, when you compare that tree with another tree, do you understand either? Or do you understand something only when there is no comparison at all?

So, is it possible to live without comparison of any kind, never translating yourself in terms of comparison with another or with some idea or with some hero or with some example? Because when you are comparing, when you are measuring yourself with 'what should be' or 'what has been', you are not seeing *what is*. Please listen to this. It is very simple, and therefore probably you, being clever, cunning, will miss it. We are asking whether it is possible to live in this world without any comparison at all. Don't say no. You have never done it. You won't say, "I cannot do it; it is impossible because all my conditioning is to compare." In a schoolroom a boy is compared with another, and the teacher says, "You are not as clever as the other." The teacher destroys B when he is comparing B with A. That process goes on through life.

— 9 —

Comparison Prevents Clarity

We think that comparison is essential for progress, for understanding, for intellectual development. I don't think it is. When you are comparing one picture with the other, you are not looking at either of them. You can only look at one picture when there is no comparison. So, in the same way, is it possible to live a life never comparing, psychologically, yourself with another? Never comparing with Rama, Sita, Gita, whoever it is, with the hero, with your gods, with your ideals. A mind that is not comparing at all, at any level, becomes extraordinarily efficient, becomes extraordinarily alive, because then it is looking at *what is*.

— 10 —

Success and Failure

As long as success is our goal we cannot be rid of fear, for the desire to succeeds inevitably breeds the fear of failure. That is why the young should not be taught to worship success. Most people seek success in one form or another, whether on the tennis court, in the business world, or in politics. We all want to be on top, and this desire creates constant conflict within ourselves and with our neighbors; it leads to competition, envy, animosity and finally to war.

Like the older generation, the young also seek success and security; though at first they may be discontented, they soon become respectable and are afraid to say no to society. The walls of their own desires begin to enclose them, and they fall in line and assume the reins of authority. Their discontent, which is the very flame of inquiry, of search, of understanding, grows dull and dies away, and in its place there comes the desire for a better job, a rich marriage, a successful career, all of which is the craving for more security.

There is no essential difference between the old and the young, for both are slaves to their own desires and gratifications. Maturity is not a matter of age, it comes with understanding. The ardent spirit of inquiry is perhaps easier for the young, because those who are older have been battered about by life, conflicts have worn them out and death in different forms awaits them. This does not mean that they are incapable of purposeful inquiry, but only that it is more difficult for them.

Many adults are immature and rather childish, and this is a contributing cause of the confusion and misery in the world...

It is security and success that most of us are after; and a mind that is seeking security, that craves success, is not intelligent, and is therefore incapable of integrated action. There can be integrated action only if one is aware of one's own conditioning, of one's racial, national, political, and religious prejudices; that is, only if one realizes that the ways of the self are ever separative.

— II —

Draw Deeply from Life

Life is a well of deep waters. One can come to it with small buckets and draw only a little water, or one can come with large vessels, drawing plentiful waters that will nourish and sustain. While one is young is the time to investigate, to experiment with everything. The school should help its young people to discover their vocations and responsibilities, and not merely cram their minds with facts and technical knowledge; it should be the soil in which they can grow without fear, happily and integrally.

CHAPTER EIGHT
Loneliness; Depression; Confusion

— 1 —

Is Loneliness the Same as Aloneness?

We know loneliness, don't we, the fear, the misery, the antagonism, the real fright of a mind that is aware of its own loneliness. We all know that. Don't we? That state of loneliness is not foreign to any one of us. You may have all the riches, all the pleasures, you may have great capacity and bliss, but within, there is always the lurking shadow of loneliness. The rich man, the poor man who is struggling, the man who is writing, creating, the worshiper—they all know this loneliness. When it is in that state, what does the mind do? The mind turns on the radio, picks up a book, runs away from *what is* into something which is not. Sirs, do follow what I am saying—not the words, but the application, the observation of your own loneliness.

When the mind is aware of its loneliness, it runs away, escapes. The escape, whether into religious contemplation or going to a cinema, is exactly the same; it is still an escape from *what is*. The man who escapes through drinking is no more immoral than the one who escapes by the worship of God; they are both the same, both are escaping. When you observe the fact that you are lonely, if there is no escape and therefore no struggle into the opposite, then generally, the mind tends to condemn it according to the frame of its knowledge, but if there is no condemnation, then the whole attitude of the mind towards the thing it has called *lonely* has undergone a complete change, has it not?

— 2 —

Loneliness Is Depression: Aloneness Is Joy

After all, loneliness is a state of isolation, because the mind encloses itself and cuts itself away from every relationship, from everything. In that state the mind knows loneliness, and if, without condemning it, the mind be aware and not create the escape, then surely that loneliness undergoes a transformation. The transformation might then be called "aloneness"—it does not matter what word you use. In that aloneness there is no fear. The mind that feels lonely because it has isolated itself through various activities is afraid of that loneliness. But if there is awareness in which there is no choice—which means no condemnation—then the mind is no longer lonely, but it is in a state of aloneness in which there is no corruption, in which there is no process of self-enclosure. One must be alone, there must be that aloneness, in that sense. Loneliness is a state of frustration, aloneness is not, and aloneness is not the opposite of loneliness.

Surely, sirs, we must be alone, alone from all influences, from all compulsions, from all demands, longings, hopes, so that the mind is no longer in the action of frustration. That aloneness is essential, it is a religious thing. But the mind cannot come to it without understanding the whole problem of loneliness. Most of us are lonely, all our activities are the activities of frustration. The happy man is not a lonely man. Happiness is alone, and the action of aloneness is entirely different from the activities of loneliness.

— 3 —

Is It Possible to Live with Loneliness?

Are we not aware of a state of emptiness in us, a state of despair, of loneliness, the complete sense of not being able to depend on anything, not having anybody to look up to? Don't we know a moment of extraordinary loneliness, of extraordinary sorrow, without reason, a sense of despair at the height of thought, at the height of love; don't we know this loneliness? And is this loneliness not pushing us always to be somebody, to be well-thought-of?

Can I live with that loneliness, not run away from it, not try to fulfill through some action? Can I live with it and not try to transform it, not try to shape and control it? If the mind can, then perhaps it will go beyond that loneliness, beyond that despair, which does not mean into hope, into a state of devotion, but on the contrary. If I can understand and live in that loneliness—not run away from it, but live in that strange loneliness which comes when I am bored, when I am afraid, when I am apprehensive, not for any cause or with cause—when I know this sense of loneliness, is it possible for the mind to live with it, without trying to push it away?

— 4 —

Dependencies End If the Mind Can Be Still

Now, if the mind can stay in that very extraordinary sense of being cut off from everything, from all ideas, from all crutches, from all dependencies, then is it not possible for such a mind to go beyond, not theoretically, but actually? It is only when it can fully experience that state of loneliness, that state of emptiness, that state of nondependency, then only is it possible...that action is not the action through the narrow funnel of the 'me'.

— 5 —

No Self, No Loneliness

The more you are conscious of yourself, the more isolated you are, and self-consciousness is the process of isolation. But aloneness is not isolation. There is aloneness only when loneliness comes to an end. Aloneness is a state in which all influence has completely ceased, both the influence from outside and the inner influence of memory; and only when the mind is in that state of aloneness can it know the incorruptible. But to come to that, we must understand loneliness, this process of isolation, which is the self and its activity. So, the understanding of the self is the beginning of the cessation of isolation, and therefore of loneliness.

— 6 —

With 6 Billion People on Earth, Is Loneliness
an Actuality or an Attitude?

Then, if we go still more deeply into it, the problem arises of
whether that which we call loneliness is an actuality or
merely a word. Is loneliness an actuality or merely a word
which covers something that may not be what we think it
is? Is not loneliness a thought, the result of thinking? That
is, thinking is verbalization based on memory, and do we
not, with that verbalization, with that thought, with that
memory, look at the state which we call "lonely?" So, the
very giving of a name to that state may be the cause of fear
which prevents us from looking at it more closely; and if we
do not give it a name, which is fabricated by the mind, then
is that state lonely?

— 7 —

Be Alone without Escapes: See What Happens

Have you ever tried to be alone? When you do try, you will
feel how extraordinarily difficult it is and how extraordinarily intelligent we must be to be alone, because the mind
will not let us be alone. The mind becomes restless, it busies
itself with escapes, so what are we doing? We are trying to
fill this extraordinary void with the known. We discover how
to be active, how to be social; we know how to study, how to
turn on the radio. We are filling that thing which we do not

know with the things we know. We try to fill that emptiness with various kinds of knowledge, relationship or things. Is that not so? That is our process, that is our existence. Now when you realize what you are doing, do you still think you can fill that void? You have tried every means of filling this void of loneliness. Have you succeeded in filling it? You have tried cinemas and you did not succeed and therefore you go after your gurus and your books or you become very active socially. Have you succeeded in filling it or have you merely covered it up? If you have merely covered it up, it is still there; therefore it will come back. If you are able to escape altogether then you are locked up in an asylum or you become very, very dull. That is what is happening in the world.

— 8 —

The Fact Is, We Are Empty

Can this emptiness, this void, be filled ? If not, can we run away from it, escape from it? If we have experienced and found one escape to be of no value, are not all other escapes therefore of no value? It does not matter whether you fill the emptiness with this or with that. So-called meditation is also an escape. It does not matter much that you change your way of escape.

How then will you find what to do about this loneliness? You can only find what to do when you have stopped escaping. Is that not so? When you are willing to face *what is*—which means you must not turn on the radio, which means you must turn your back to civilization—then that loneliness comes to an end, because it is completely transformed. It is no longer loneliness.

— 9 —

Depression : Life Lived inside the Self

Questioner: What is the difference between awareness and introspection? And who is aware in awareness?

Krishnamurti: Let us first examine what we mean by introspection. We mean by introspection looking within oneself, examining oneself. Why does one examine oneself? In order to improve, in order to change, in order to modify. You introspect in order to become something, otherwise you would not indulge in introspection. You would not examine yourself if there were not the desire to modify, change, to become something other than what you are. That is the obvious reason for introspection. I am angry and I introspect, examine myself, in order to get rid of anger or to modify or change anger. Where there is introspection, which is the desire to modify or change the responses, the reactions of the self, there is always an end in view; when that end is not achieved there is moodiness, depression. Therefore introspection invariably goes with depression.

— 10 —
Self-Analysis Brings Depression

I don't know if you have noticed that when you introspect, when you look into yourself in order to change yourself, there is always a wave of depression. There is always a moody wave which you have to battle against; you have to examine yourself again in order to overcome that mood and so on. Introspection is a process in which there is no release because it is a process of transforming *what is* into something which it is not. Obviously that is exactly what is taking place when we introspect, when we indulge in that peculiar action. In that action, there is always an accumulative process, the 'I' examining something in order to change it. So there is always a dualistic conflict and therefore a process of frustration. There is never a release; and realizing that frustration, there is depression.

Awareness is entirely different. Awareness is observation without condemnation. Awareness brings understanding, because there is no condemnation or identification but silent observation. If I want to understand something, I must observe, I must not criticize, I must not condemn, I must not pursue it as pleasure or avoid it as non-pleasure. There must merely be the silent observation of a fact. There is no end in view but awareness of everything as it arises. That observation and the understanding of that observation cease when there is condemnation, identification, or justification.

— II —

Introspection or Awareness?

Introspection is self-improvement and therefore introspection is self-centeredness. Awareness is not self-improvement. On the contrary, it is the ending of the self, of the 'I', with all its peculiar idiosyncrasies, memories, demands and pursuits. In introspection there is identification and condemnation. In awareness there is no condemnation or identification; therefore there is no self-improvement. There is a vast difference between the two.

The man who wants to improve himself can never be aware. Because improvement implies condemnation and the achievement of a result. Whereas in awareness there is observation without condemnation, without denial or acceptance. That awareness begins with outward things, being aware, being in contact with objects, with nature. First, there is awareness of things about one, being sensitive to objects, to nature, then to people, which means relationship; then .there is awareness of ideas. This awareness, being sensitive to things, to nature, to people, to ideas, is not made up of separate processes, but is one unitary process. It is a constant observation of everything, of every thought and feeling and action as they arise within oneself.

— 12 —
Do We Need Psychoanalysts to Solve Our Confusion?

Questioner: It is now a well-established fact that many of our diseases are psychosomatic, brought on by deep inner frustrations and conflicts of which we are often unaware. Must we now run to psychiatrists as we used to run to physicians, or is there a way for man to free himself from this inner turmoil?

Krishnamurti: Which raises the question: What is the position of the psychoanalysts? And what is the position of those of us who have some form of disease or illness? Is the disease brought on by our emotional disturbances, or is it without emotional significance? Most of us are disturbed. Most of us are confused, in turmoil, even the very prosperous who have refrigerators, cars, and all the rest of it; and as we do not know how to deal with the disturbance, inevitably it reacts on the physical and produces an illness, which is fairly obvious. And the question is: Must we run to psychiatrists to help us to remove our disturbances and thereby regain health, or is it possible for us to find out for ourselves how not to be disturbed, how not to have turmoil, anxieties, fears?

Why are we disturbed, if we are? What is disturbance? I want something, but I can't get it, so I'm in a state. I want to fulfill through my children, through my wife, through my property, through position, success, and all the rest of it, but

I am blocked, which means that I am disturbed. I am ambitious, but somebody else pushes me aside and gets ahead; again I am in chaos, in turmoil, which produces its own physical reaction.

— 13 —
What Is Confusion?

Now, can you and I be free of all this turmoil and confusion? Do you understand? What is confusion? Confusion exists only when there is the fact plus what I think about the fact: my opinion about the fact, my disregard of the fact, my evasion of the fact, my evaluation of the fact, and so on. If I can look at the fact without the additive quality, then there is no confusion. If I recognize the fact that a certain road leads to Ventura, there is no confusion. Confusion arises only when I think or insist that the road leads somewhere else—and that is actually the state that most of us are in.

— 14 —
Our Opinions Confuse the Facts

Our opinions, our beliefs, our desires, ambitions, are so strong, we are so weighed down by them, that we are incapable of looking at the fact.

So, the fact plus opinion, judgment, evaluation, ambition, and all the rest of it, brings about confusion. And can you and I, being confused, not act? Surely, any action born of confusion must lead to further confusion, further turmoil, all of which reacts on the body, on the nervous system, and produces illness. Being confused, to acknowledge to oneself that one is confused requires, not courage, but a certain clarity of thought, clarity of perception. Most of us are afraid to acknowledge that we are confused, so out of our confusion we choose leaders, teachers, politicians; and when we choose something out of our confusion, that very choice must be confused, and therefore the leader must also be confused.

— 15 —

Understanding Confusion Is Clarity

Is it possible, then, to be aware of our confusion, and to know the cause of that confusion, and not act? When confused mind acts, it can only produce further confusion; but a mind that is aware that it is confused and understands this whole process of confusion need not act because that very clarity is its own action. I think this is rather difficult for most people to understand because we are so used to acting, doing...

— 16 —
You Can See All This for Yourself

And I do not think any analyst can solve this problem. He may temporarily help you to conform to a certain pattern of society which he calls normal existence, but the problem is much deeper than that, and no one can solve it except yourself. You and I have made this society; it is the result of our actions, of our thoughts, of our very being, and as long as we are merely trying to reform the product without understanding the entity that has produced it, we shall have more diseases, more chaos, more delinquency. The understanding of the self brings about wisdom and right action.

CHAPTER NINE

Self-Ending—Not Self-Improvement— Ends Suffering

— I —

Why Strengthen the Very Source of Your Pain?

One of the most difficult things to understand, it seems to me, is this problem of change. We see that there is progress in different forms, so-called evolution, but is there a funda-mental change in progress? I do not know if this problem has struck you at all, or whether you have ever thought about it, but perhaps it will be worthwhile to go into the question this morning.

We see that there is progress in the obvious sense of that word; there are new inventions, better cars, better planes, better refrigerators, the superficial peace of a progressive society, and so on. But does that progress bring about a radical change in man, in you and me? It does superficially alter the conduct of our life, but can it ever fundamentally transform our thinking? And how is this fundamental transformation to be brought about? I think it is a problem worth considering. There is progress in self-improvement—I can be better tomorrow, more kind, more generous, less envious, less ambitious. But does self-improvement bring about a complete change in one's thinking? Or is there no change at all, but only progress? Progress implies time, does it not? I am this today, and I shall be something better tomorrow. That is, in self-improvement or self-denial or self-abnegation, there is progression, the gradualism of moving towards a better life, which means superficially adjusting to environment, conforming to an improved pattern, being conditioned in a nobler way, and so on. We see that process taking place all the time. And you must have wondered, as I have, whether progress does bring about a fundamental revolution.

To me, the important thing is not progress but revolution. Please don't be horrified by that word *revolution*, as most people are in a very progressive society like this. But it seems to me that unless we understand the extraordinary necessity of bringing about not just a social amelioration but a radical change in our outlook, mere progress is progress in sorrow; it may effect the pacification, the calming of sorrow, but not the cessation of sorrow, which is always latent. After all, progress in the sense of getting better over a period of time is really the process of the self, the 'me', the ego. There is progress in self-improvement, obviously, which is the determined effort to be good, to be more this or less that, and so on. As there is improvement in refrigerators and airplanes, so also there is improvement in the self, but that improvement, that progress, does not free the mind from sorrow.

— 2 —

Don't Just Redecorate Your Prison

So, if we want to understand the problem of sorrow and perhaps put an end to it, then we cannot possibly think in terms of progress because a man who thinks in terms of progress, of time, saying that he will be happy tomorrow, is living in sorrow. And to understand this problem, one must go into the whole question of consciousness, must one not? Is this too difficult a subject? I'll go on and we'll see.

If I really want to understand sorrow and the ending of sorrow, I must find out, not only what are the implications of progress, but also what that entity is who wants to improve himself, and I must also know the motive with which he seeks to improve. All this is consciousness. There is the superficial consciousness of everyday activity: the job, the family, the constant adjustment to social environment, either happily, easily, or contradictorily, with a neurosis. And there is also the deeper level of consciousness, which is the vast social inheritance of man through centuries...

We are trying to discover for ourselves what is consciousness, and whether it is possible for the mind to be free of sorrow—not to change the pattern of sorrow, not to decorate the prison of sorrow, but to be completely free from the seed, the root of sorrow. In inquiring into that, we shall see the difference between progress and the psychological revolution which is essential if there is to be freedom from sorrow.

— 3 —

Observe the Seat of Sorrow: Your Own Consciousness

We are not trying to alter the conduct of our consciousness; we are not trying to do something about it; we are just looking at it. Surely, if we are at all observant, slightly aware of anything, we know the superficial consciousness. We can see that on the surface our mind is active, occupied in adjustment, in a job, earning a livelihood, in expressing certain tendencies, gifts, talents, or acquiring certain technical knowledge; and most of us are satisfied to live on that surface.

— 4 —

Why Do We Accept the Pain of Superficial Living?

Now, can we go below that and see the motive of this superficial adjustment? Again, if you are a little aware of this whole process, you know that this adjustment to opinion, to values, this acceptance of authority and so on, is motivated by self-perpetuation, self-protection. If you can go still below that, you will find there is this vast undercurrent of racial, national, and group instincts, all the accumulations of human struggle, knowledge, endeavor, the dogmas and traditions of the Hindu, the Buddhist, or the Christian, the residue of so-called education through centuries—all of which has conditioned the mind to a certain inherited pattern. And if you can go deeper still, there is the primal desire to be, to succeed, to become, which expresses itself on the surface in various forms of social activity and creates deep-rooted anxieties, fears. Put very succinctly, the whole of that is our consciousness. In other words, our thinking is based on this fundamental urge to be, to become, and on top of that lie the many layers of tradition, of culture, of education, and the superficial conditioning of a given society—all forcing us to conform to a pattern that enables us to survive. There are many details and subtleties, but in essence that is our consciousness.

— 5 —

Sorrow Does Not End through Improvement

Now, any progress within that consciousness is self-improvement, and self-improvement is progress in sorrow, not the cessation of sorrow. This is quite obvious if you look at it. And if the mind is concerned with being free of all sorrow, then what is the mind to do? I do not know if you have thought about this problem, but please think about it now.

We suffer, don't we? We suffer, not only from physical illness, disease, but also from loneliness, from the poverty of our being; we suffer because we are not loved. When we love somebody and there is no loving in return, there is sorrow. In every direction, to think is to be full of sorrow: therefore, it seems better not to think, so we accept a belief and stagnate in that belief, which we call religion.

Now, if the mind sees that there is no ending of sorrow through self-improvement through progress, which is fairly obvious, then what is the mind to do? Can the mind go beyond this consciousness, beyond these various urges and contradictory desires? And is going beyond a matter of time? Please follow this, not merely verbally, but actually. If it is a matter of time, then you are back again in the other thing, which is progress. Do you see that? Within the framework of consciousness, any movement in any direction is self-improvement and therefore the continuance of sorrow. Sorrow may be controlled, disciplined, subjugated, rationalized, superrefined, but the potential quality of sorrow is still there;

and to be free from sorrow there must be freedom from this potentiality, from this seed of the 'I', the self, from the whole process of becoming. To go beyond, there must be the cessation of this process.

— 6 —

Through Progress Sorrow Does Not End

But if you say, "How am I to go beyond?" then the 'how ' becomes the method, the practice, which is still progress, therefore there is no going beyond but only the refinement of consciousness in sorrow. I hope you are getting this.

The mind thinks in terms of progress, of improvement, of time; and is it possible for such a mind, seeing that so-called progress is progress in sorrow, to come to an end—not in time, not tomorrow, but immediately? Otherwise you are back again in the whole routine, in the old wheel of sorrow. If the problem is stated clearly and clearly understood, then you will find the absolute answer.

— 7 —

Dying to Everything Day to Day

Now, to go beyond, to transcend all that, requires tremendous attention. This total attention, in which there is no choice, no sense of becoming, of changing, altering, wholly frees the mind from the process of self-consciousness; there is then no experiencer who is accumulating, and it is only then that the mind can be truly said to be free from sorrow. It is accumulation that is the cause of sorrow. We do not die to everything from day to day; we do not die to the innumerable traditions, to the family, to our own experiences, to our own desire to hurt another. One has to die to all that from moment to moment, to that vast accumulative memory, and only then the mind is free from the self, which is the entity of accumulation.

SECTION THREE

Education, Work, and Money

CHAPTER ONE

What Is Education?

— I —

The Right Kind of Education

The ignorant man is not the unlearned, but he who does not know himself, and the learned man is stupid when he relies on books, on knowledge, and on authority to give him understanding. Understanding comes only through self-knowledge, which is awareness of one's total psychological process. Thus education, in the true sense, is the understanding of oneself, for it is within each one of us that the whole of existence is gathered.

What we now call education is a matter of accumulating information and knowledge from books, which anyone can do who can read. Such education offers a subtle form of escape from ourselves and, like all escapes, it inevitably creates increasing misery. Conflict and confusion result from our own wrong relationship with people, things and ideas, and until we understand that relationship and alter it, mere learning, the gathering of facts and the acquiring of various skills, can only lead us to engulfing chaos and destruction.

As society is now organized, we send our children to school to learn some technique by which they can eventually earn a livelihood. We want to make the child first and foremost a specialist, hoping thus to give him a secure economic position. But does the cultivation of a technique enable us to understand ourselves?

While it is obviously necessary to know how to read and write, and to learn engineering or some other profession, will technique give us the capacity to understand life? Surely, technique is secondary; and if technique is the only thing we are striving for, we are obviously denying what is by far the greater part of life.

Life is pain, joy, beauty, ugliness, love, and when we understand it as a whole, at every level, that understanding creates its own technique. But the contrary is not true: technique can never bring about creative understanding.

— 2 —

Skill In Making a Living Is Not Living Completely

Present-day education is a complete failure because it has over-emphasized technique. In over-emphasizing technique we destroy man. To cultivate capacity and efficiency without understanding life, without having a comprehensive perception of the ways of thought and desire, will only make us increasingly ruthless, which is to engender wars and jeopardize our physical security. The exclusive cultivation of technique has produced scientists, mathematicians, bridge builders, space conquerors; but do they understand the total process of life? Can any specialist experience life as a whole? Only when he ceases to be a specialist.

— 3 —

Mere Occupation Is not Enough

Technological progress does solve certain kinds of problems for some people at one level, but it introduces wider and deeper issues too. To live at one level, disregarding the total process of life, is to invite misery and destruction. The greatest need and most pressing problem for every individual is to have an integrated comprehension of life, which will enable him to meet its ever-increasing complexities.

Technical knowledge, however necessary, will in no way resolve our inner, psychological pressures and conflicts; and it is because we have acquired technical knowledge without understanding the total process of life that technology has become a means of destroying ourselves. The man who knows how to split the atom but has no love in his heart becomes a monster.

We choose a vocation according to our capacities; but will the following of a vocation lead us out of conflict and confusion? Some form of technical training seems necessary; but when we have become engineers, physicians, accountants— then what? Is the practice of a profession the fulfillment of life? Apparently with most of us it is. Our various professions may keep us busy for the greater part of our existence; but the very things that we produce and are so entranced with are causing destruction and misery. Our attitudes and values make of things and occupations the instruments of envy, bitterness and hate.

Without understanding ourselves, mere occupation leads to frustration, with its inevitable escapes through all kinds of mischievous activities.

— 4 —

The Individual or the System

Education should not encourage the individual to conform to society or to be negatively harmonious with it, but help him to discover the true values which come with unbiased investigation and self-awareness. When there is no self-knowledge, self-expression becomes self-assertion, with all its aggressive and ambitious conflicts. Education should awaken the capacity to be self-aware and not merely indulge in gratifying self-expression.

What is the good of learning if in the process of living we are destroying ourselves? As we are having a series of devastating wars, one right after another, there is obviously something radically wrong with the way we bring up our children. I think most of us are aware of this, but we do not know how to deal with it.

Systems, whether educational or political, are not changed mysteriously; they are transformed when there is a fundamental change in ourselves. The individual is of first importance, not the system; and as long as the individual does not understand the total process of himself, no system, whether of the left or of the right, can bring order and peace to the world.

— 5 —

The Function of Education

The right kind of education is concerned with individual freedom, which alone can bring true cooperation with the whole, with the many; but this freedom is not achieved through the pursuit of one's own aggrandizement and success. Freedom comes with self-knowledge, when the mind goes above and beyond the hindrances it has created for itself through craving its own security.

It is the function of education to help each individual to discover all these psychological hindrances, and not merely impose upon him new patterns of conduct, new modes of thought. Such impositions will never awaken intelligence, creative understanding, but will only further condition the individual. Surely, this is what is happening throughout the world, and that is why our problems continue and multiply.

— 6 —

Are Our Children Our Property?

It is only when we begin to understand the deep significance of human life that there can be true education; but to understand, the mind must intelligently free itself from the desire for reward which breeds fear and conformity. If we regard our children as personal property, if to us they are the continuance of our petty selves and the fulfillment of our ambitions, then we shall build an environment, a social structure in which there is no love, but only the pursuit of self-centered advantages.

— 7 —

What Is Our Necessity?

What is our necessity? According to that, you will have universities, schools, examinations or no examinations. But to merely talk narrowly about linguistic divisions seems to me utterly infantile. What we will have to do as mature human beings—if there are such entities existing—is to go into this problems. Do you want your children to be educated to be glorified clerks, bureaucrats, leading utterly miserable, useless, futile lives, functioning as machines in a system? Or, do you want integrated human beings who are intelligent, capable, fearless? We will find out, probably, what we mean by "intelligence." The mere acquisition of knowledge is not intelligence, and it does not make an intelligent human being. You may have all the technique, but that does not necessarily mean that you are an intelligent, integrated human being.

— 8 —

Knowledge Is Accumulation of the Past:
Learning Is Always in the Present

So, there is a difference between acquiring knowledge and the act of learning. You must have knowledge and the act of learning. You must have knowledge; otherwise you will not know where you live, you will forget your name, and so on. So at one level knowledge is imperative, but when that knowledge is used to understand life—which is a movement, which is a thing that is living, moving, dynamic, every moment changing—when you cannot move with life, then you are living in the past and trying to comprehend the extraordinary thing called life. And to understand life, you have to learn every minute about it and never come to it having learned.

CHAPTER TWO

Comparison and Competition, or Cooperation?

— 1 —

Comparison Breeds Fear

One of the things that prevents the sense of being secure is comparison. When you are compared with somebody else in your studies or in your games or in your looks, you have a sense of anxiety, a sense of fear, a sense of uncertainty. So, as we were discussing yesterday with some of the teachers, it is very important to eliminate in our school this sense of comparison, this giving grades or marks, and ultimately the fear of examinations...

You study better when there is freedom, when there is happiness, when there is some interest. You all know that when you are playing games, when you are doing dramatics, when you are going out for walks, when you are looking at the river, when there is general happiness, good health, then you learn much more easily. But when there is fear of comparison, of grades, of examinations, you do not study or learn so well...

The teacher is concerned only that you should pass examinations and go to the next class, and your parents want you to get a class ahead. Neither of them is interested that you should leave the school as an intelligent human being without fear.

— 2 —

Competition

Questioner: I would like not to be competitive, but how is one to exist without competing in this highly competitive society?

Krishnamurti: You see, we take it for granted that we must live in this competing society, so there is a premise laid down, and from there we start. As long as you say, "I must live in this competing society," you will be competitive. This society is acquisitive; it worships success, and if you also want to be successful, naturally you must be competitive.

But the problem is much deeper and more significant than mere competition. What lies behind the desire to compete? In every school we are taught to compete, are we not? Competition is exemplified by the giving of marks, by comparing the dull boy with the clever boy, by endlessly pointing out that the poor boy may become the president or the head of General Motors—you know the whole business. Why do we lay so much stress on competition? What is the significance behind it? For one thing, competition implies discipline, does it not? You must control, you must conform, you must toe the line, you must be like all the others, only better, so you discipline yourself in order to succeed. Please follow this. Where there is the encouragement of competition, there must also be the process of disciplining the mind to a certain pattern of action, and is that not one of the ways of controlling the boy or the girl? If you want to become something, you must control, discipline, compete. We have been brought up on that, and we pass it on to our children. And yet we talk about giving the child freedom to find out, to discover!

Competition hides the state of one's own being. If you want to understand yourself, will you compete with another, will you compare yourself with anyone? Do you understand yourself through comparison? Do you understand anything through comparison, through judgment? Do you understand a painting by comparing it with another painting or only when your mind is completely aware of the picture without comparison?

— 3 —

Competition Only Hides Fear of Failure

You encourage the spirit of competition in your son because you want him to succeed where you have failed; you want to fulfill yourself through your son or through your country. You think that progress, evolution, lies through judgment, through comparison, but when do you compare, when do you compete? Only when you are uncertain of yourself, when you do not understand yourself, when there is fear in your heart. To understand oneself is to understand the whole process of life, and self-knowledge is the beginning of wisdom. But without self-knowledge, there is no understanding; there is only ignorance, and the perpetuation of ignorance is not growth.

— 4 —

Competition Is the Worship of an Outward Show

So, does it require competition to understand oneself? Must I compete with you in order to understand myself? And why this worship of success? The man who is uncreative, who has nothing in himself—it is he who is always reaching out, hoping to gain, hoping to become something, and as most of us are inwardly poor, inwardly poverty-stricken, we compete in order to become outwardly rich. The outward show of comfort, of position, of authority, of power, dazzles us because that is what we want.

— 5 —

Cooperation Is the Absence of Self-Centeredness

There can be cooperation only when you and I are as nothing. Find out what it means, think it out and meditate about it. Don't just ask questions. What does that state of nothingness mean? What do you mean by it? We only know the state of activity of the self, the self-centered activity...

So, we know that there cannot be fundamental cooperation though there may be superficial persuasion through fear, through reward, through punishment, and so on—which is not cooperation obviously.

So, where there is activity of the self as the end in view, as the utopia in view—that is nothing but destruction, separation, and there is no cooperation. What is one to do if one is really desirous, or one wants really to find out, not superficially but really, and bring about cooperation? If you want cooperation from your wife, your child, or your neighbor, how do you set about it? You set about by loving the person. Obviously!

Love is not a thing of the mind; love is not an idea. Love can be only when the activity of the self has ceased to be. But you call the activity of the self positive; that positive act leads to destruction, separativeness, misery, confusion, all of which you know so well and so thoroughly. And yet, we all talk of cooperation, brotherhood. Basically, we want to cling to our activities of the self.

— 6 —
Is It All about Me—or Us?

So, a man who really wants to pursue and find out the truth of cooperation must inevitably bring to an end the self-centered activity. When you and I are not self-centered, we love each other; then you and I are interested in action, and not in the result, not in the idea but in doing the action; you and I have love for each other. When my self-centered activity clashes with your self-centered activity, then we project an idea towards which we both quarrel; superficially we are cooperating, but we are at each other's throats all the time.

So, to be nothing is not the conscious state, and when you and I love each other, we cooperate, not to do something about which we have an idea, but in whatever there is to be done.

If you and I loved each other, do you think the dirty, filthy villages would exist? We would act; we would not theorize and would not talk about brotherhood. Obviously, there is no warmth or sustenance in our hearts, and we talk about everything; we have methods, systems, parties, governments, and legislations. We do not know that words cannot capture that state of love.

The word *love* is not love. The word *love* is only the symbol, and it can never be the real. So, don't be mesmerized by that word *love*.

— 7 —

Know when Not to Cooperate

When you know how to cooperate because there is this inward revolution, then you will also know when not to cooperate, which is really very important, perhaps more important. We now cooperate with any person who offers a reform, a change, which only perpetuates conflict and misery: but if we can know what it is to have the spirit of cooperation that comes into being with the understanding of the total process of the self, then there is a possibility of creating a new civilization, a totally different world in which there is no acquisitiveness, no envy, no comparison. This is not a theoretical utopia but the actual state of mind that is constantly inquiring and pursuing that which is true and blessed.

CHAPTER THREE

Work: How Do You Decide?

— I —

Your Life Must Not Destroy Another

Don't you want to find out if it is possible to live in this world richly, fully, happily, creatively, without the destructive drive of ambition, without competition? Don't you want to know how to live so that your life will not destroy another or cast a shadow across his path?

You see, we think this is a utopian dream which can never be brought about in fact; but I am not talking about utopia;

that would be nonsense. Can you and I, who are simple, ordinary people, live creatively in this world without the drive of ambition which shows itself in various ways as the desire for power, position? You will find the right answer when you love what you are doing. If you are an engineer merely because you must earn a livelihood, or because your father or society expects it of you, that is another form of compulsion; and compulsion in any form creates a contradiction, conflict. Whereas if you really love to be an engineer, or a scientist, or if you can plant a tree, or paint a picture, or write a poem, not to gain recognition but just because you love to do it, then you will find that you never compete with another. I think this is the real key: to love what you do.

— 2 —
Find out What You Love

But when you are young it is often very difficult to know what you love to do, because you want to do so many things. You want to be an engineer, a locomotive driver, an airplane pilot zooming along in the blue skies; or perhaps you want to be a famous orator or politician. You may want to be an artist, a chemist, a poet or a carpenter. You may want to work with your head, or do something with your hands. Is any of these things what you really love to do, or is your interest in them merely a reaction to social pressures? How can you find out? And is not the true purpose of education to *help* you to find out, so that as you grow up you can begin to give your whole mind, heart and body to that which you really love to do?

To find out what you love to do demands a great deal of intelligence; because, if you are afraid of not being able to earn a livelihood, or of not fitting into this rotten society, then you will never find out. But, if you are not frightened, if you refuse to be pushed into the groove of tradition by your parents, by your teachers, by the superficial demands of society, then there is a possibility of discovering what it is you really love to do. So, to discover, there must be no fear of not surviving.

But most of us are afraid of not surviving. We say, "What will happen to me if I don't do as my parents say, if I don't fit into this society?" Being frightened, we do as we are told, and in that there is no love, there is only contradiction; and this inner contradiction is one of the factors that bring about destructive ambition.

So, it is a basic function of education to help you to find out what you really love to do, so that you can give your whole mind and heart to it, because that creates human dignity, that sweeps away mediocrity, the petty bourgeois mentality. That is why it is important to have the right teachers...

— 3 —

Teaching Is the Noblest Profession

Teaching is the noblest profession—if it can be called a pro-fession at all. It is an art that requires, not just intellectual attainments, but infinite patience and love. To be truly edu-cated is to understand our relationship to all things—to money, to property, to people, to nature—in the vast field of our existence.

— 4 —

The Howling Mess

Questioner: In your book on education you suggest that mod-ern education is a complete failure. I would like you to explain this.

Krishnamurti: Is it not a failure, sir? When you go out on the street you see the poor man and the rich man; and when you look around you, you see all the so-called educated people throughout the world wrangling, fighting, killing each other in wars. There is now scientific knowledge enough to enable us to provide food, clothing and shelter for all hu-man beings, yet it is not done. The politicians and other leaders throughout the world are educated people, they have titles, degrees, caps and gowns, they are doctors and scien-tists; and yet they have not created a world in which man can live happily. So modern education has failed, has it not? And if you are satisfied to be educated in the same old way, you will make another howling mess of life.

— 5 —

Are You Putty?

Questioner: May I know why we should not fit into our parents' plans, since they want us to be good?

Krishnamurti: Why should you fit into your parents' plans, however worthy, however noble they may be? You are not just putty, you are not jelly to be fitted into a mold. And if you do fit in, what happens to you? You become a so-called good girl, or good boy, and then what? Do you know what it means to be good? Goodness is not just doing what society says, or what your parents say. Goodness is something entirely different, is it not? Goodness comes into being only when you have intelligence, when you have love, when you have no fear. You cannot be good if you are afraid. You can become respectable by doing what society demands—then society gives you a garland, it says what a good person you are; but merely being respectable is not being good.

You see, when we are young we do not want to fit in, and at the same time we want to be good. We want to be nice, to be sweet, we want to be considerate and do kind things; but we do not know what it all means, and we are 'good' because we are afraid. Our parents say, "Be good," and most of us are good, but such 'goodness' is merely living according to their plans for us.

— 6 —
What Is Right Livelihood?

Questioner: What are the foundations of right livelihood? How can I find out whether my livelihood is right, and how am I to find right livelihood in a basically wrong society?

Krishnamurti: In a basically wrong society, there cannot be right livelihood. What is happening throughout the world at the present time? Whatever livelihood we have brings us to war, to general misery and destruction, which is an obvious fact. Whatever we do inevitably leads to conflict, to decay, to ruthlessness and sorrow. So the present society is basically wrong; it is founded—is it not?—on envy, hate, and the desire for power, and such a society is bound to create wrong means of livelihood, such as the soldier, the policeman, and the lawyer. By their very nature, they are a disintegrating factor in society, and the more lawyers, policemen, and soldiers there are, the more obvious the decay of society. That is what is happening throughout the world: there are more soldiers, more policemen, more lawyers, and naturally the business man goes with them. All that has to be changed in order to found a right society—and we think such a task is impossible. It is not, but it is you and I who have to do it. Because at present whatever livelihood we undertake either creates misery for another, or leads to the ultimate destruction of mankind, which is shown in our daily existence. How can that be changed? It can be changed only when you and I are not seeking power, are not envious, are not full of hatred and antagonism. When you, in your relationship, bring about transformation, then you are helping to create a new society, a society in which there are people who are not held by tradition, who do not ask anything for themselves, who are not pursuing power, because inwardly they are rich, they have found reality. Only the man who seeks reality can create a new society; only the man who loves can bring about a transformation in the world.

— 7 —

Do the Best You Can: You Must Eat

I know this is not a satisfactory answer for a person who wants to find out what is the right livelihood in the present structure of society. You must do the best you can in the present structure of society—either become a photographer, a merchant, a lawyer, a policeman, or whatever it is. But if you do, be conscious of what you are doing, be intelligent, be aware, fully cognizant, of what you are perpetuating, recognize the whole structure of society, with its corruption, with its hatred, with its envy; and if you yourself do not yield to these things, then perhaps you will be able to create a new society. But the moment you ask what is right livelihood, all these questions are inevitably there, are they not? You are not satisfied with your livelihood; you want to be envied, you want to have power, you want to have greater comforts and luxuries, position and authority, and therefore you are inevitably creating or maintaining a society that will bring destruction upon man, upon yourself.

If you clearly see that process of destruction in your own livelihood, if you see that it is the result of your own pursuit of livelihood, then obviously you will find the right means of earning money. But first you must see the picture of society as it is, a disintegrating, corrupted society; and when you see it very clearly, then your means of earning a livelihood will come. But first you must see the picture, see the world as it is, with its national divisions, with its cruelties, ambitions, hatreds, and controls. Then, as you see it more clearly, you will find that a right means of livelihood comes into being—you don't have to seek it. But the difficulty with most of us is that we have too many responsibilities; fathers, mothers are waiting for us to earn money and support them. And as it is difficult to get a job the way society is at the present time, any job is welcome; so we fall into the machinery of society. But those who are not so compelled, who have no need of an immediate job and can therefore look at the whole picture, it is they who are responsible. But you see, those who are not concerned with an immediate job are caught up in something else—they are concerned with their self-expansion, with their comforts, with their luxuries, with their amusements. They have time, but are dissipating it. And those who have time are responsible for the alteration of society; those who are not immediately pressed for a livelihood should really concern themselves with this whole problem of existence, and not get entangled in mere political action, in superficial activities. Those who have time and so-called leisure should seek out truth, because it is they who can bring about a revolution in the world, not the man whose stomach is empty. But, unfortunately, those who have leisure are not occupied with the eternal. They are occupied in filling their time. Therefore they also are a cause of misery and confusion in the world. So those of you who are listening, those of you who have a little time, should give thought and consideration to this problem, and by your own transformation you will bring about a world revolution

— 8 —

What Is Livelihood?

Sirs, what do we mean by livelihood? It is the earning of one's needs—food, clothing, shelter—is it not? The difficulty of livelihood arises only when we use the essentials of life, food, clothing, shelter as a means of psychological aggression. That is, when we use the needs, the necessities, as means of self-aggrandizement, using the essentials as a psychological expansion of oneself.

— 9 —
Give Back

All that one can do, if one is earnest, if one is intelligent about this whole process, is to reject the present state of things and give to society all that one is capable of. That is, sir, you accept food, clothing, and shelter from society, and you must give something to society in return...

Now, what are you giving to society? What is society? Society is relationship with one or with many; it is your relationship with another. What are you giving to another? Are you giving anything to another in the real sense of the word, or merely taking payment for something?...

You are not depending on another for your psychological needs—and it is only then that you can have a right means of livelihood.

You may say this is all a very complicated answer, but it is not. Life has no simple answer. The man who looks for a simple answer to life has obviously a dull mind, a stupid mind. Life has no conclusion, life has no definite pattern; life is living, altering, changing...

If your relationship is one of need and not of greed, then you will find the right means of livelihood where you are, even when society is corrupt.

— 10 —

The True Work of Man Is to Discover Truth

So, what is the true work of man? Surely, the true work of man is to discover truth, God; it is to love and not to be caught in his own self-enclosing activities. In the very discovery of what is true there is love, and that love in man's relationship with man will create a different civilization, a new world.

What Is the Basis for Right Action?

— I —

Why Change Ourselves at All?

First of all, why do we want to change *what is*, or bring about a transformation? Why? Because what we are dissatisfies us; it creates conflict, disturbance; and disliking that state, we want something better, something nobler, more idealistic. So, we desire transformation because there is pain, discomfort, conflict.

— 2 —
For One Thing, We Are Boring

The activities of the self are frighteningly monotonous. The self is a bore; it is intrinsically enervating, pointless, futile. Its opposing and conflicting desires, its hopes and frustration, its realities and illusions are enthralling, and yet empty; its activities lead to its own weariness. The self is ever climbing and ever falling down, ever pursuing and ever being frustrated, ever gaining and ever losing; and from this weary round of futility it is ever trying to escape. It escapes through outward activity or through gratifying illusions, through drink, sex, radio, books, knowledge, amusements, and so on. Its power to breed illusion is complex and vast.

— 3 —
The Problem of the Self Cannot Be Solved through Escape

Self-forgetfulness is sought within and without; some turn to religion, and others to work and activity. But there is no means of forgetting the self. The inner or outward noise can suppress the self, but it soon comes up again in a different form; for what is suppressed must find a release. Self-forgetfulness through drink or sex, through worship or knowledge, makes for dependence, and that on which you depend creates a problem.

— 4 —

A Problem Is Never Solved on Its Own Level

Problems will always exist where the activities of the self are dominant. To be aware which are and which are not activities of the self needs constant vigilance...

A problem is never solved on its own level; being complex, it must be understood in its total process. To try to solve a problem on only one level, physical or psychological, leads to further conflict and confusion. For the resolution of a problem, there must be this awareness, this passive alertness which reveals its total process.

— 5 —

The Position of Youth in Relationship to Problems

I don't think the problems of youth, middle age, and old age can be separated; youth has not a special problem. It may appear that way because the young are just beginning their lives. Either we make a mess of our lives right from the start, and so are caught in a morass of problems, uncertainties, dissatisfactions, and despair, or when we are young—and I think that perhaps is the only time—we lay a right foundation...

So, it seems to me that when one is young, when one is uncommitted to a family, a job, and all the activities and miseries, it is then that one can begin to sow a seed that will blossom right throughout one's life, instead of getting lost in all the meaningless and absurd pursuits of our daily existence.

— 6 —
Molding of the Mind Is Conditioning

You know, we are always told what to think and what not to think. Books, teachers, parents, the society around us, all tell us what to think, but they never help us to find out *how* to think. To know *what* to think is comparatively easy, because from early childhood our minds are conditioned by words, by phrases, by established attitudes and prejudices. I do not know if you have noticed how the minds of most older people are fixed; they are set like clay in a mold, and it is very difficult to break through this mold. This molding of the mind is conditioning.

— 7 —
Problem-Solving, Right Action, Is Listening to Life as It Changes, Not Memorizing Rules

It is *understanding* that is creative, not memory, not remembrance. Understanding is the liberating factor, not the things that you have stored up in your mind...

Life is something that you listen to, that you understand from moment to moment, without accumulating experience...Like the river, life is running, swift, volatile, never still; and when you meet life with the heavy burden of memory, naturally you are never in contact with life...There is no new thing as long as we are burdened with memories; and life being everlastingly new, we cannot understand it. Therefore our living is very tedious; we become lethargic, we grow mentally and physically fat and ugly.

— 8 —

Right Action Is Not Obedience (Which Does Not Mean Disregarding Traffic Laws, Courtesies, Public Welfare)

Whatever our age, most of us obey, follow, copy, because we are inwardly frightened of being uncertain. We want to be certain, both financially and morally; we want to be approved of. We want to be in a safe position, to be enclosed and never to be confronted with trouble, pain, suffering...It is fear of being punished that prevents us from doing something harmful to others.

— 9 —

Understand for Yourself All the Problems of Life

When we grow older and leave school after receiving a so-called education, we have to face many problems. What profession are we to choose, so that in it we can fulfill ourselves and be happy? In what vocation or job will we feel that we are not exploiting or being cruel to others? We have to face the problems of suffering, disaster, death. We have to understand starvation, over-population, sex, pain, pleasure. We have to deal with the many confusing and contradictory things in life: the wrangles between man and man, between man and woman; the conflicts within and the struggles without. We have to understand ambition, war, the military spirit—and that extraordinary thing called peace, which is much more vital than we realize. We have to comprehend the significance of religion, which is not mere speculation or the worship of images, and also that very strange and complex thing called love. We have to be sensitive to the beauty of life, to a bird in flight—and also to the beggar, to the squalor of the poor, to the hideous buildings that people put up, to the foul road and the still fouler temple. We have to face all these problems. We have to face the question of whom to follow or not to follow, and whether we should follow anyone at all.

Most of us are concerned with bringing about a little change here and there, and with that we are satisfied. The older we grow, the less we want any deep, fundamental change, because we are afraid. We do not think in terms of total transformation, we think only in terms of superficial change; and if you look into it you will find that superficial change is no change at all. It is not a radical revolution, but merely a modified continuity of what has been. All these things you have to face from your own happiness and misery to the happiness and misery of the many; from your own ambitions and self-seeking pursuits to the ambitions, motivations and pursuits of others. You have to face competition, the corruption in yourself and in others, the deterioration of the mind, the emptiness of the heart. You have to know all this, you have to face and understand it for yourself.

— 10 —

No Thinker Has Solved Your Problems

Thinking has not solved our problems. The clever ones, the philosophers, the scholars, the political leaders, have no really solved any of our human problems—which are the relationship between you and another, between you and myself.

— 11 —

Intelligence Is Freedom from Self

Intelligence is possible only when there is real freedom from the self, from the 'me', that is, when the mind is no longer the center of the demand for the 'more', no longer caught up in the desire for the greater, wider, more expansive experience.

— 12 —

Do Not Meet Violence with Violence

When you leave school and enter college, and later face the world, it seems to me that what is important is not to succumb, not to bow your heads to various influences, but to meet and understand these as they are and see their true significance and their worth, in a gentle spirit with great inward strength which will not create further discord in the world.

SECTION FOUR

Relationships

CHAPTER ONE
What Is Relationship?

— I —

Are We in Relationship—or Only Our Images?

What do we mean by that word *relationship?* Are we ever related to anyone, or is the relationship between two images which we have created about each other? I have an image about you, and you have an image about me. I have an image about you as my wife or husband, or whatever it is, and you an image about me also. The relationship is between these two images and nothing else. To have relationship with another is only possible when there is no image. When I can look at you and you can look at me without the image of memory, of insults, and all the rest, then there is a relationship, but the very nature of the observer is the image, isn't it? My image observes your image, if it is possible to observe it, and this is called relationship, but it is between two images, a relationship which is nonexistent because both are images. To be related means to be in contact. Contact must be something direct, not between two images. It requires a great deal of attention, an awareness, to look at another without the image which I have about that person, the image being my memories of that person—how he has insulted me, pleased me, given me pleasure, this or that. Only when there are no images between the two is there a relationship.

— 2 —

Relationship Is Not Dependency

Now, for most of us, relationship with another is based on dependence, economic or psychological. This dependence creates fear, breeds in us possessiveness, results in friction, suspicion, frustration. Economic dependence on another can perhaps be eliminated through legislation and proper organization, but I am referring especially to that psychological dependence on another which is the outcome of craving for personal satisfaction, happiness, and so on. One feels, in this possessive relationship, enriched, creative, and active; one feels one's own little flame of being is increased by another and so in order not to lose this source of completeness, one fears the loss of the other, and so possessive fears come into being with all their resulting problems. Thus, in this relationship of psychological dependence, there must always be conscious or unconscious fear, suspicion, which often lies hidden in pleasant-sounding words. The reaction of this fear leads one ever to search for security and enrichment through various channels, or to isolate oneself in ideas and ideals, or to seek substitutes for satisfaction.

Though one is dependent on another, there is yet the desire to be inviolate, to be whole. The complex problem in relationship is how to love without dependence, without friction and conflict; how to conquer the desire to isolate oneself, to withdraw from the cause of conflict. If we depend for our happiness on another, on society, or on environment, they become essential to us; we cling to them and any alteration of these we violently oppose because we depend upon them for our psychological security and comfort. Though, intellectually, we may perceive that life is a continual process of flux, mutation, necessitating constant change, yet emotionally or sentimentally we cling to the established and comforting values; hence there is a constant battle between change and the desire for permanency. Is it possible to put an end to this conflict?

— 3 —

Can We Love and yet Not Possess?

Life cannot be without relationship, but we have made it so agonizing and hideous by basing it on personal and possessive love. Can one love and yet not possess? You will find the true answer not in escape, ideals, beliefs but through the understanding of the causes of dependence and possessiveness. If one can deeply understand this problem of relationship between oneself and another, then perhaps we shall understand and solve the problems of our relationship with society, for society is but the extension of ourselves.

— 4 —

Personal Relationships Create All Society

The environment which we call society is created by past generations; we accept it, as it helps us to maintain our greed, possessiveness, illusion. In this illusion there cannot be unity or peace. Mere economic unity brought about through compulsion and legislation cannot end war. As long as we do not understand individual relationship, we cannot have a peaceful society. Since our relationship is based on possessive love, we have to become aware, in ourselves, of its birth, its causes, its action. In becoming deeply aware of the process of possessiveness with its violence, fears, its reactions, there comes an understanding that is whole, complete. This understanding alone frees thought from dependence and possessiveness. It is within oneself that harmony in relationship can be found, not in another, nor in environment.

— 5 —

Look to Yourself, Not the Other, to Solve Conflicts

In relationship, the primary cause of friction is oneself, the self that is the center of unified craving. If we can but realize that it is not how another acts that is of primary importance, but how each one of us acts and reacts, and if that reaction and action can be fundamentally, deeply understood, then relationship will undergo a deep and radical change. In this relationship with another, there is not only the physical problem but also that of thought and feeling on all levels, and one can be harmonious with another only when one is harmonious integrally with oneself. In relationship the important thing to bear in mind is not the other but oneself, which does not mean that one must isolate oneself but understand deeply in oneself the cause of conflict and sorrow. So long as we depend on another for our psychological wellbeing, intellectually or emotionally, that dependence must inevitably create fear from which arises sorrow.

— 6 —

Life Is Relationship with Things, People, Ideas

Life is relationship with things, people, and ideas, and if we do not meet these relationships rightly, fully, then conflicts arise from the impact of the challenge.

— 7 —

The Mirror of Relationship

Relationship, surely, is the mirror in which you discover yourself. Without relationship, you are not; to be is to be related; to be related is existence. And you exist only in relationship; otherwise, you do not exist, existence has no meaning. It is not because you think you are that you come into existence. You exist because you are related, and it is the lack of understanding of relationship that causes conflict.

— 8 —

The Key to Happiness Is Self-Knowledge in Relationship

You are already understanding yourself in the mirror of your own thoughts, in the mirror of relationship…I feel that happiness lies in our own hands, and the key to that happiness is self-knowledge—not the self-knowledge of Freud, or Jung, or Shankara, or somebody else, but the self-knowledge of your own discovery in your relationship from day to day...Through observation, through awareness without effort of the movement of your own thought from day to day, as you get into a bus, while you are riding in a car, when you are talking to...your wife, to your children, to your neighbor—through observing all that as in a mirror, you begin to discover how you talk, how you think, how you react, and you will find that in understanding yourself you have something which cannot be found in books, in philosophies, in the teachings of any guru.

— 9 —

Stop the Image-Making Machinery

So, to establish right relationship is to destroy the image...you have to destroy the machinery that creates the image—the machinery that is in you and the machinery that is in the other. Otherwise you may destroy one image, and the machinery will create another image.

— 10 —

How Does the Image, the Opinion, Begin?

One has to go into and find out how the image comes into being and if it is possible to stop the machinery that creates it. Then only is there relationship between human beings— it will not be between two images, which are dead entities.

It is very simple. You flatter me, you respect me; and I have an image about you, through insult through flattery. I have experience—pain, death, misery, conflict, hunger, loneliness. All that creates an image in me; I am that image. Not that I am the image, not that the image and I are different; but the 'I' is that image; the thinker is that image. It is the thinker that creates the image. Through his responses, through his reactions—physical, psychological, intellectual, and so on— the thinker, the observer, the experiencer, creates that image through memory, through thought. So the machinery is thinking, the machinery comes into existence through thought. And thought is necessary, otherwise you cannot exist.

So, first see the problem. Thought creates the thinker. The thinker begins to create the image about himself...He creates the image and he lives in it. So thinking is the beginning of this machinery. And you will say, "How can I stop thinking?" You cannot. But one can think and not create the image.

— II —

Opinions Are Just Images

And naturally there is no relationship between images. If you have an opinion about me and if I have an opinion about you, how can we have any relationship? Relationship exists only when it is free, when there is freedom from this image-formation.

— 12 —

Self-Image Leads to Pain

Why are you hurt? Self-importance, is it not? And why is there self-importance?

Because one has an idea, a symbol of oneself, an image of oneself, what one should be, what one is or what one should not be. Why does one create an image about oneself?...What awakens anger is that our ideal, the idea we have of ourselves, is attacked. And our idea about ourselves is our escape from the fact of what we are. But when you are observing the actual fact of what you are, no one can hurt you. Then, if one is a liar and is told that one is a liar it does not mean that one is hurt; it is a fact.

CHAPTER TWO

Love; Desire; Sex; Dependency

— I —

Where There Is Dependency, Attachment, There Is No Love

Psychologically, then, our relationships are based on dependence, and that is why there is fear. The problem is not how
not to depend, but just to see the fact that we do depend.
Where there is attachment there is no love. Because you do
not know who to love, you depend, and hence there is fear.

What is important is to see that fact, and not ask how to love, or how to be free from fear.

— 2 —

Where There Is Dependency, There Is Fear

Without refuting, accepting, or giving opinions about it, without quoting this or that, just listen to the fact that where there is attachment there is no love, and where there is dependency there is fear. I am talking of psychological dependency, not of your dependence on the milkman to bring you milk, or your dependence on the railway, or on a bridge. It is this inward psychological dependency on ideas, on people, on property, that breeds fear.

— 3 —

Love Comes in Understanding Relationship

Love is something that cannot be cultivated; love is not a thing to be bought by the mind. If you say, "I am going to practice being compassionate," then compassion is a thing of the mind, and therefore not love. Love comes into being darkly, unknowingly, fully, when we understand this whole process of relationship. Then the mind is quiet; it does not fill the heart with things of the mind, and therefore that which is love can come into being.

— 4 —

Why Have We Made Sex so Important?

What do we mean by the problem of sex? Is it the act, or is it a thought about the act? Surely, it is not the act. The sexual act is no problem to you any more than eating is a problem to you, but if you think about eating or anything else all day long because you have nothing else to think about, it becomes a problem to you...Why do you build it up, which you are obviously doing? The cinemas, the magazines, the stories, the way women dress: everything is building up your thoughts of sex. And why does the mind build it up; why does the mind think about sex at all? Why, sirs and ladies? It is your problem. Why?

Why has it become a central issue in your life? When there are so many things calling, demanding your attention, you give complete attention to the thought of sex. What happens; why are your minds so occupied with it? Because that is a way of ultimate escape, is it not? It is a way of complete self-forgetfulness.

For the time being, at least for the moment, you can forget yourself—and there is no other way of forgetting yourself. Everything else you do in life gives emphasis to the 'me', to the self. Your business, your religion, your gods, your leaders, your political and economic actions, your escapes, your social activities, your joining one party and rejecting another—all that is emphasizing and giving strength to the 'me'....When there is only one thing in your life that is an avenue to ultimate escape, to complete forget-fulness of yourself if only for a few seconds, you cling to it because that is the only moment you are happy…

So, sex becomes an extraordinarily difficult and complex problem as long as you do not understand the mind that thinks about the problem.

— 5 —

Why Is Sex a Problem?

Why is it that whatever we touch we turn into a problem?…Why has sex become a problem? Why do we submit to living with problems; why do we not put an end to them? Why do we not die to our problems instead of car-rying them day after day, year after year? Surely, sex is a relevant question, which I shall answer presently, but there is the primary question: why do we make life into a prob-lem? Working, sex, earning money, thinking, feeling, experiencing, you know, the whole business of living—why is it a problem? Is it not essentially because we always think from a particular point of view, from a fixed point of view?

— 6 —

Desire Is Not Love

Desire is not love; desire leads to pleasure; desire is pleasure. We are not denying desire. It would be utterly stupid to say that we must live without desire, for that is impossible. Man has tried that. People have denied themselves every kind of pleasure, disciplined themselves, tortured themselves, and yet desire has persisted, creating conflict, and all the brutalizing effects of that conflict. We are not advocating desirelessness, but we must understand the whole phenomena of desire, pleasure, and pain, and if we can go beyond, there is a bliss and ecstasy which is love.

CHAPTER THREE

Family and Society:
Relationship or Exclusion?

— I —

Family and Society

The family is against society; the family is against human relationship as a whole. You know, it is like living in one part of a big house, in one little room, and making an extraordinary thing of that one little room, which is the family. The family has only importance in relation to the whole of the house. As that one room is in relation to the whole of the house, so is the family in relation to the whole of human existence. But we separate it; we cling to it. We make much about the family—my relations and your relations—and we battle with each other everlastingly. And the family is like the little room in relation to the whole house. When we forget the whole house, then the little room becomes terribly important; so also the family becomes very important when you forget the whole of human existence. The family has only importance in relation to the whole of human existence; otherwise, it becomes a dreadful thing, a monstrous thing...

— 2 —

Do We Truly Love Our Families?

And when we say, "We love the family," we do not really love that family; we do not love our children—actually we do not. When you say that you love your children, you really mean that they have become a habit, toys—things of amusement for a while. But, if you love something, your children, then you would care.

You know what caring is? If you care, when you plant a tree, you care for it; you cherish it; you nourish it...You have to dig deep before you plant, then see the soil is right, then plant, then protect it, then watch it every day, look after it as if it were a part of your whole being. But you do not love the children that way. If you did, then you would have a different kind of education altogether. There would be no wars, there would be no poverty. The mind then would not be trained to be merely technical. There would be no competition, there would be no nationality. And because we do not love, all this has been allowed to grow.

— 3 —

Depending Makes You Incapable

When you say you love somebody, don't you depend on him? It is all right when you are young to be dependent on your father, on your mother, on your teacher, or on your guardian. Because you are young, you need to be looked after, you need clothes, you need shelter, you need security. While you are young, you need a sense of being held together, of somebody looking after you. But even as you grow older, this feeling of dependence remains, does it not? Have you not noticed it in older people, in your parents and your teachers? Have you not noticed how they depend on their wives, on their children, on their mothers? People when they grow up still want to hold on to somebody, still feel that they need to be dependent. Without looking to somebody, without being guided by somebody, without a feeling of comfort and security in somebody, they feel lonely, do they not? They feel lost. So, this dependency on another is called love, but if you watch it more closely, you will see dependency is fear; it is not love. Because they are afraid to be alone, because they are afraid to think things out for themselves, because they are afraid to feel, to watch, to find out the whole meaning of life, they feel they love God. So they depend on what they call God, but a thing created by the mind is not dependable; it is not God, the unknown. It is the same with an ideal or a belief. I believe in something, and that gives me great comfort...

It is right that you should do so when you are young, but if you keep on depending when you have grown to maturity, that will make you incapable of thinking, of being free. Where there is dependence there is fear, and where there is fear there is authority; there is no love...

— 4 —

It Is Natural to Have a Family: To Hide There Is Catastrophe

The family as it is now is a unit of limited relationship, self-enclosing and exclusive...We must understand the desire for inward, psychological security and not merely replace one pattern of security with another.

So the problem is not the family, but the desire to be secure. Is not the desire for security, at any level, exclusive? This spirit of exclusiveness shows itself as the family, as property, as the State, the religion, and so on. Does not this desire for inward security build up outward forms of security which are always exclusive? The very desire to be secure destroys security. Exclusion, separation, must inevitably bring about disintegration; nationalism, class-antagonism, and war, are its symptoms. The family as a means of inward security is a source of disorder and social catastrophe.

— 5 —

The Only Security Is Learning to
Live without Inward Security

It is only when we do not seek inward security that we can live outwardly secure...

Using another as a means of satisfaction and security is not love. Love is never security; love is a state in which there is no desire to be secure; it is a state of vulnerability; it is the only state in which exclusiveness, enmity, and hate are impossible. In that state a family may come into being, but it will not be exclusive, self-enclosing.

Nature and Earth

— 1 —

What Is Our Relationship with Nature?

Sir, I do not know if you have discovered your relationship with nature. There is no "right" relationship, there is only the understanding of relationship. Right relationship implies the mere acceptance of a formula, as does right thought. Right thought and right thinking are two different things. Right thought is merely conforming to what is right, what is respectable, whereas right thinking is movement, it is the product of understanding, and understanding is constantly undergoing modification, change. Similarly, there is a difference between right relationship and understanding our relationship with nature. What is your relationship with nature?—nature being the rivers, the trees, the swift-flying birds, the fish in the water, the minerals under the earth, the waterfalls and shallow pools. What is your relationship to them? Most of us are not aware of that relationship. We never look at a tree, or if we do, it is with a view of using that tree— either to sit in its shade or to cut it down for lumber. In other words, we look at trees with a utilitarian purpose; we never look at a tree without projecting ourselves and utilizing it for our own convenience.

— 2 —

Do We Love Our Earth, or Just Use It as We Do Each Other?

We treat the earth and its products in the same way. There is no love of earth, there is only usage of earth. If one really loved the earth, there would be frugality in using the things of the earth. That is, sir, if we were to understand our relationship with the earth, we should be very careful in the use we made of the things of the earth. The understanding of one's relationship with nature is as difficult as understanding one's relationship with one's neighbor, wife, and children. But we have not given a thought to it, we have never sat down to look at the stars, the moon, or the trees.

We are too busy with social or political activities. Obviously, these activities are escapes from ourselves, and to worship nature is also an escape from ourselves. We are always using nature, either as an escape or for utilitarian ends—we never actually stop and love the earth or the things of the earth. We never enjoy the rich fields, though we utilize them to feed and clothe ourselves. We never like to till the earth with our hands—we are ashamed to work with our hands.

— 3 —

Maps Are Political Opinions, Not Facts:
the Earth Is Not 'Yours' and 'Mine'

So, we have lost our relationship with nature. If once we understood that relationship, its real significance, then we would not divide property into yours and mine; though one might own a piece of land and build a house on it, it would cease to be 'mine' or 'yours' in the exclusive sense—it would be more a means of taking shelter. Because we do not love the earth and the things of the earth but merely utilize them, we are insensitive to the beauty of a waterfall, we have lost the touch of life, we have never sat with our backs against the trunk of a tree; and since we do not love nature, we do not know how to love human beings and animals.

— 4 —

We Are Caretakers—Each of Us Temporary at That

It does not mean that you cannot use the earth, but you must use the earth as it is to be used. Earth is there to be loved and cared for, not to be divided as 'yours' and 'mine'. It is foolish to plant a tree in a compound and call it 'mine'.

CHAPTER FIVE

Marriage: Love and Sex

— 1 —

Is Marriage Mutual Use?

Now, do you call it love when in your relationship with your wife there is possessiveness, jealousy, fear, constant nagging, dominating, and asserting? Can that be called love? When you possess a person and thereby create a society which helps you to possess the person, do you call that love? When you use somebody for your sexual convenience or in any other way, do you call that love? Obviously it is not. That is, where there is jealousy, where there is fear, where there is possessiveness, there is no love. Surely, love does not admit of contention, of jealousy. When you possess, there is fear and though you may call it love, it is far from love. Experience it, sirs and ladies, as we go along. You are married and have children; you have wives or husbands whom you possess, whom you use, of whom you are afraid or jealous. Be aware of that and see if it is love.

— 2 —

Love Cannot Be Thought About

You can think about a person whom you love, but you cannot think about love. Love cannot be thought about; though you may identify yourself with a person, a country, a church, the moment you think about love, it is not love—it is merely mentation…Because the mind is active, it fills the empty heart with the things of the mind; and with these things of the mind we play, we create problems…The problems are the product of the mind, and for the mind to solve its own problem it has to stop, for only when the mind stops is there love.

— 3 —

When You Know How to Love One
You Know How to Love the Whole

Love cannot be thought about, love cannot be cultivated, love cannot be practiced. The practice of love, the practice of brotherhood, is still within the field of the mind; therefore, it is not love. When all this has stopped, then love comes into being, then you will know what it is to love. Then love is not quantitative, but qualitative. You do not say, "I love the whole world," but when you know how to love one, you know how to love the whole. Because we do not know how to love one, our love of humanity is fictitious. When you love, there is neither one nor many—there is only love. It is only when there is love that all our problems can be solved, and then we shall know its bliss and its happiness.

— 4 —

Love in Relationship

Love in relationship is a purifying process as it reveals the ways of the self.

How easy it is to destroy the thing we love! How quickly a barrier comes between us, a word, a gesture, a smile! Health, mood, and desire cast a shadow, and what was bright becomes dull and burdensome. Through usage we wear ourselves out, and that which was sharp and clear becomes wearisome and confused. Through constant friction, hope and frustration, that which was beautiful and simple becomes fearful and expectant. Relationship is complex and difficult, and few can come out of it unscathed. Though we would like it to be static, enduring, continuous, relationship is a movement, a process which must be deeply and fully understood and not made to conform to an inner or outer pattern. Conformity, which is the social structure, loses its weight and authority only when there is love. Love is a purifying process as it reveals the ways of the self. Without this revelation, relationship has little significance.

— 5 —

We Do Not Love; We Crave to Be Loved

But how we struggle against this revelation! The struggle takes many forms: dominance or subservience, fear or hope, jealousy or acceptance, and so and on. The difficulty is that we do not love; and if we *do* love we want it to function in a particular way, we do not give it freedom. We love with our minds and not with our hearts. Mind can modify itself, but love cannot. Mind can make itself invulnerable, but love cannot; mind can always withdraw, be exclusive, become personal or impersonal. Love is not to be compared and hedged about. Our difficulty lies in that which we *call* love, which is really of the mind. We fill our hearts with the things of the mind and so keep our hearts ever empty and expectant. It is the mind that clings, that is envious, that holds and destroys. Our life is dominated by the physical centers and by the mind. We do not love and let it alone, but crave to be loved; we give in order to receive, which is the generosity of the mind and not of the heart. The mind is ever seeking certainty, security; and can love be made certain by the mind? Can the mind, whose very essence is of time, catch love, which is its own eternity?

But even the love of the heart has its own tricks; for we have so corrupted our heart that it is hesitant and confused. It is this that makes life so painful and wearisome. One moment we think we have love, and the next it is lost. There comes an imponderable strength, not of the mind, whose sources may not be fathomed. This strength is again destroyed by the mind; for in this battle the mind seems invariably to be the victor. This conflict within ourselves is not to be resolved by the cunning mind or by the hesitant heart. There is no means, no way to bring this conflict to an end. The very search for a means is another urge of the mind to be the master, to put away conflict in order to be peaceful, to have love, to become something.

— 6 —

Love Is Not Yours or Mine

Our greatest difficulty is to be widely and deeply aware that there is no means to love as a desirable end of the mind.

When we understand this really and profoundly, then there is a possibility of receiving something that is not of this world. Without the touch of that something, do what we will, there can be no lasting happiness in relationship. If you have received that benediction and I have not, naturally you and I will be in conflict. You may not be in conflict, but I will be; and in my pain and sorrow I cut myself off. Sorrow is as exclusive as pleasure, and until there is that love which is not of my making, relationship is pain. If there is the benediction of that love, you cannot but love me whatever I may be, for then you do not shape love according to my behavior.

— 7 —

What Makes Us Stale in Relationship?

If you observe, what makes us stale in our relationship is thinking, calculating, judging, weighing, adjusting ourselves; and the one thing that frees us from that is love, which is not a process of thought.

— 8 —

When There Is No Love, We Invent Marriage

When there is no love, then the framework of marriage as an institution becomes a necessity. When there is love, then sex is not a problem—it is the lack of love that makes it into a problem. Don't you know? When you love somebody really deeply—not with the love of the mind, but really from your heart—you share with him or her everything that you have, not your body only, but everything. In your trouble, you ask her help and she helps you. There is no division between man and woman when you love somebody, but there is a sexual problem when you do not know that love.

— 9 —

Gratification Is Not the Flame of Love

Questioner: You have talked about relationship based on usage of another for one's own gratification, and you have often hinted at a state called love. What do you mean by love?

Krishnamurti: We know what our relationship is—a mutual gratification and use, though we clothe it by calling it love. In usage there is tenderness for and the safeguarding of what is used. We safeguard our frontier, our books, our property; similarly, we are careful in safeguarding our wives, our families, our society, because without them we would be lonely, lost. Without the child, the parent feels lonely; what you are not, the child will be, so the child becomes an instrument of your vanity. We know the relationship of need and usage. We need the postman and he needs us, yet we don't say we love the postman. But we do say that we love our wives and children, even though we use them for our personal gratification and are willing to sacrifice them for the vanity of being called patriotic. We know this process very well, and obviously, it cannot be love. Love that uses, exploits, and then feels sorry, cannot be love because love is not a thing of the mind.

Now, let us experiment and discover what love is—discover, not merely verbally, but by actually experiencing that state. When you use me as a guru and I use you as disciple, there is mutual exploitation. Similarly, when you use your wife and children for your furtherance, there is exploitation. Surely, that is not love. When there is use, there must be possession; possession invariably breeds fear, and with fear come jealousy, envy, suspicion. When there is usage, there cannot be love, for love is not something of the mind. To think about a person is not to love that person. You think about a person only when that person is not present, when he is dead, when he has run off, or when he does not give you what you want. Then your inward insufficiency sets the process of the mind going. When that person is close to you, you do not think of him; to think of him when he is close to you is to be disturbed, so you take him for granted—he is there. Habit is a means of forgetting and being at peace so that you won't be disturbed. So, usage must invariably lead to invulnerability, and that is not love.

What is that state when usage—which is thought process as a means to cover the inward insufficiency, positively or negatively—is not? What is that state when there is no sense of gratification? Seeking gratification is the very nature of the mind. Sex is sensation which is created, pictured by the mind, and then the mind acts or does not act. Sensation is a process of thought, which is not love. When the mind is dominant and the thought process is important, there is no love. This process of usage, thinking, imagining, holding, enclosing, rejecting, is all smoke, and when the smoke is not, the flame of love is. Sometimes we do have that flame, rich, full, complete; but the smoke returns...

— 10 —

Don't Debate Opposites: Neither Celibacy nor Promiscuity

Those who are trying to be celibate in order to achieve God are unchaste for they are seeking a result or gain and so substituting the end, the result, for sex—which is fear. Their hearts are without love...Only when the mind and heart are unburdened of fear, of the routine of sensational habits, when there is generosity and compassion, there is love. Such love is chaste.

— 11 —

Why Is It that Sex and Marriage Have Become Such Problems?

How is it possible to meet the sexual demand intelligently and not turn it into a problem?

Now, what do we mean by sex? The purely physical act, or the thought that excites, stimulates, furthers that act? Surely, sex is of the mind, and because it is of the mind, it must seek fulfillment, or there is frustration...

Why is it that sex has become such a problem in our lives? Let us go into it, not with constraint, not with anxiety, fear, condemnation. Why has it become a problem? Surely, for most of you it is a problem. Why? Probably, you have never asked yourself why it is a problem. Let us find out.

Sex is a problem because it would seem that in that act there is a complete absence of the self. In that moment you are happy because there is the cessation of self-consciousness, of the 'me'; and desiring more of it—more of the abnegation of the self in which there is complete happiness through full fusion, integration, naturally it becomes all-important. Isn't that so? Because it is something that gives me unadulterated joy, complete self-forgetfulness, I want more and more of it. Now, why do I want more of it? Because everywhere else I am in conflict, everywhere else, at all the different levels of existence, there is the strengthening of the self. Economically, socially, religiously, there is the constant thickening of self-consciousness, which is conflict. After all, you are self-conscious only when there is conflict. Self-consciousness is in its very nature the result of conflict. So, everywhere else we are in conflict. In all our relationships with property, with people, with ideas there is conflict, pain, struggle, misery; but in this one act there is complete cessation of all that. Naturally you want more of it because it gives you happiness, while all the rest leads you to misery, turmoil, conflict, confusion, antagonism, worry, destruction; therefore, the sexual act becomes all-significant, all-important.

So, the problem is not sex, surely, but how to be free from the self...

Sirs, the self is not an objective entity that can be studied under the microscope or learned through books or understood through quotations, however weighty those quotations may be. It can be understood only in relationship. After all, conflict is in relationship, whether with property, with an idea, with your wife, or with your neighbor; and without solving that fundamental conflict, merely to hold onto that one release through sex, is obviously to be unbalanced. And that is exactly what we are. We are unbalanced because we have made sex the one avenue of escape; and society, so-called modern culture, helps us to do it. Look at the advertisements, the cinemas, the suggestive gestures, postures, appearances.

Most of you married when you were quite young, when the biological urge was very strong. You took a wife or a husband, and with that wife or husband you jolly well have to live for the rest of your life. Your relationship is merely physical, and everything else has to be adjusted to that. So what happens? You are intellectual, perhaps, and she is very emotional. Where is your communion with her? Or she is very practical, and you are dreamy, vague, rather indifferent. Where is the contact between you and her when you use her? Our marriages are now based on that idea, on that urge; but more and more there are contradictions and great conflicts in marriage, and so divorces.

So, this problem requires intelligent handling, which means that we have to alter the whole basis of our education; and that demands understanding not only the facts of life but also our everyday existence, not only knowing and understanding the biological urges, the sexual urge, but also seeing how to deal with it intelligently.

— 12 —

Insight Sees the Limits of Thought In All of This

Mercy and pity, forgiveness and respect are not emotions. There is love when sentimentality and emotion and devotion cease. Devotion is not love; devotion is a form of self-expansion. Respect is not for the few, but for man, whether he is low or high. Generosity and mercy have no reward.

Love alone can transform insanity, confusion, and strife. No system, no theory of the left or of the right can bring peace and happiness to man. Where there is love, there is no possessiveness, no envy; there is mercy and compassion, not in theory, but actually to your wife and to your children, to your neighbor...

There is love with its blessing when 'you' cease to be.

— 13 —
Can Love Be Fixed, Static?

An experience of pleasure makes us demand more of it, and the 'more' is this urge to be secure in our pleasures. If we love someone, we want to be quite sure that that love is returned, and we seek to establish a relationship which we at least hope will be permanent. All our society is based on that relationship. But is there anything which is permanent? Is there? Is love permanent? Our constant desire is to make sensation permanent, is it not? And the thing which cannot be made permanent, which is love, passes us by.

— 14 —
In Considering Marriage:
Where You Are Important, Love Is Not

We are trying to understand the problem of marriage, in which is implied sexual relationship, love, companionship, communion. Obviously if there is no love, marriage becomes a disgrace, does it not? Then it becomes mere gratification. To love is one of the most difficult things, is it not? Love can come into being, can exist only when the self is absent. Without love, relationship is a pain; however gratifying, or however superficial, it leads to boredom, to routine, to habit with all its implications. Then, sexual problems become all important. In considering marriage, whether it is necessary or not, one must first comprehend love. Surely love is chaste; without love you cannot *be* chaste; you may be a celibate, whether a man or a woman, but that is not being chaste, that is not being pure, if there is no love. If you have an ideal of chastity, that is if you want to become chaste, there is no love in it either because it is merely the desire to become something which you think is noble, which you think will help you to find reality; there is no love there at all. Licentiousness is not chaste, it leads only to degradation, to misery. So does the pursuit of an ideal. Both exclude love, both imply becoming something, indulging in something; and therefore you become important, and where you are important, love is not.

— 15 —

In Habit There Is No Love

Marriage as a habit, as a cultivation of habitual pleasure, is a deteriorating factor, because there is no love in habit.

It is only for the very, very few who love that the married relationship has significance, and then it is unbreakable, then it is not mere habit or convenience, nor is it based on biological, sexual need. In that love which is unconditional the identities are fused, and in such a relationship there is a remedy, there is hope.

But for most of you, the married relationship is not fused. To fuse the separate identities, you have to know yourself, and she has to know herself. That means to love. But there is no love, which is an obvious fact. Love is fresh, new, not mere gratification, not mere habit. It is unconditional. You don't treat your husband or wife that way, do you? You live in your isolation, and she lives in her isolation, and you have established your habits of assured sexual pleasure. What happens to a man who has an assured income? Surely, he deteriorates. Have you not noticed it? Watch a man who has an assured income and you will soon see how rapidly his mind is withering away. He may have a big position, a reputation for cunning, but the full joy of life is gone out of him.

Similarly, you have a marriage in which you have a permanent source of pleasure, a habit without understanding, without love, and you are forced to live in that state. I am not saying what you should do, but look at the problem first. Do you think this is right? It does not mean that you must throw off your wife and pursue someone else. What does this relationship mean? Surely, to love is to be in communion with somebody, but are you in communion with your wife, except physically? Do you know her, except physically? Does she know you? Are you not both isolated, each pursuing his or her own interests, ambitions, and needs, each seeking from the other gratification, economic or psychological security? Such a relationship is not a relationship at all—it is a mutually self-enclosing process of psychological, biological, and economic necessity—and the obvious result is conflict, misery, nagging, possessive fear, jealousy, and so on.

So marriage as a habit, as a cultivation of habitual plea-sure, is a deteriorating factor because there is no love in habit. Love is not habitual; love is something joyous, creative, new.

CHAPTER SIX
Passion

— 1 —

Without Passion, Life Is Empty

For most of us, passion is employed only with regard to one thing, sex; or you suffer passionately and try to resolve that suffering. But I am using the word passion in the sense of a state of mind, a state of being, a state of your inward core, if there is such a thing, that feels very strongly, that is highly sensitive— sensitive alike to dirt, to squalor, to poverty, and to enormous riches and corruption, to the beauty of a tree, of a bird, to the flow of water, and to a pond that has the evening sky reflected upon it. To feel all this intensely, strongly, is necessary. Because without passion life becomes empty, shallow, and without much meaning. If you cannot see the beauty of a tree and love that tree, if you cannot care for it intensely, you are not living.

— 2 —

How Can You Love Unless You Are Passionate?

You cannot be sensitive if you are not passionate. Do not be afraid of that word passion. Most religious books, most gurus, swamis, leaders, and all the rest of them say, "Don't have passion." But if you have no passion, how can you be sensitive to the ugly, to the beautiful, to the whispering leaves, to the sunset, to a smile, to a cry? How can you be sensitive without a sense of passion in which there is abandonment? Sirs, please listen to me, and do not ask how to acquire passion. I know you are all passionate enough in getting a good job, or hating some poor chap, or being jealous of someone; but I am talking of something entirely different—a passion that loves. Love is a state in which there is no "me," love is a state in which there is no condemnation, no saying that sex is right or wrong, that this is good and something else is bad. Love is none of these contradictory things. Contradiction does not exist in love. And how can one love if one is not passionate? Without passion, how can one be sensitive?

To be sensitive is to feel your neighbor sitting next to you; it is to see the ugliness of the town with its squalor, its filth, its poverty, and to see the beauty of the river, the sea, the sky. If you are not passionate, how can you be sensitive to all that? How can you feel a smile, a tear? Love, I assure you, is passion.

— 3 —

Passion Is Dangerous

It is only a mind that is learning that is very passionate. We are using the word *passion* not in a sense of heightened pleasure but rather that state of mind that is always learning and, therefore, always eager, alive, moving, vital, vigorous, young, and therefore passionate. Very few of us are passionate. We have sensual pleasures—lust, enjoyment—but the sense of passion most of us have not. Without passion, in the large sense or meaning of that word, how can you learn, how can you discover new things, how can you inquire, how can you run with the movement of inquiry?

And a mind that is very passionate is always in danger. Perhaps most of us, unconsciously, are aware of this passionate mind which is learning and therefore acting, and have failed unconsciously; and probably that is one of the reasons why we are never passionate. We are respectable, we conform. We accept, we obey. There is respectability, duty, and all the rest of those words which we use to smother the act of learning.

— 4 —

Keep Learning: Don't Be Stuck in a Groove

This act of learning, we said, is discipline. This discipline has no conformity of any kind and therefore no suppression because when you are learning about your feelings, about your anger, about your sexual appetites, and other things, there is no occasion to suppress, there is no occasion to indulge. And this is one of the most difficult things to do because all our tradition, all the past, all the memory, the habits, have set the mind in a particular groove, and we follow easily in the groove, and we do not want to be disturbed in any way from that groove. Therefore, for most of us, discipline is merely conformity, suppression, imitation, ultimately leading to a very respectable life—if it is at all life. A man caught within the framework of respectability, of suppression, of imitation, conformity—he does not live at all; all he has learned, all he has acquired is an adjustment to a pattern; and the discipline which he has followed has destroyed him.

CHAPTER SEVEN
Truth; God; Death

— I —

What Do We Mean by Death?

Death awaits each one of us, whether we like it or not. You may be a high government official with titles, wealth, position, and a red carpet, but there is this inevitable thing at the end of it. So what do we mean by death? By death we obviously mean putting an end to continuity, do we not? There is a physical death, and we a little bit anxious about it, but that does not matter if we can overcome it by continuing in some other form. So when we ask about death, we are concerned with whether there is continuity or not. And what is the thing that continues? Obviously, not your body because every day we see that people who die are burned or buried.

— 2 —

What Continues?

Therefore, we mean, do we not, a supersensory continuity, a psychological continuity, a thought continuity, a continuity of character, which is termed the soul, or what you will. We want to know if thought continues. That is, I have meditated, I have practiced so many things, I have not finished writing my book, I have not completed my career, I am weak and need time to grow strong, I want to continue my pleasure, and so on—and I am afraid that death will put an end to all that. So, death is a form of frustration, is it not? I am doing something, and I don't want to end it; I want continuity in order to fulfill myself. Now, is there fulfillment through continuity? Obviously, there is fulfillment of a sort through continuity. If I am writing a book, I don't want to die until I have finished it; I want time to develop a certain character, and so on.

— 3 —

So, there is fear of death only when there is the desire to fulfill oneself because to fulfill oneself, there must be time, longevity, continuity. But if you can fulfill yourself from moment to moment, you are not afraid of death.

Now, our problem is how to have continuity in spite of death, is it not? And you want an assurance from me, or, if I don't assure you of that, you go to somebody else, to your gurus, to your books, or to various other forms of distraction and escape. So, you listening to me and I talking to you, we are going to find out together what we actually mean by continuity, what it is that continues—and what we want to continue. That which continues is obviously a wish, a desire, is it not? I am not powerful but I would like to be; I have not built my house but I would like to build it; I have not got that title but I would like to get it; I have not amassed enough money but I will do so presently; I would like to find God in this life—and so on and on. So, continuity is the process of want. When this is put an end to, you call it death, do you not? You want to continue desire as a means of achievement, as a process through which to fulfill yourself. Surely, this is fairly simple, is it not?

— 4 —

Thought Continues

Now, obviously, thought continues in spite of your physical death. This has been proved. Thought is a continuity because, after all, what are you? You are merely a thought, are you not? You are the thought of a name, the thought of a position, the thought of money; you are merely an idea. Remove the idea, remove the thought, where are you? So, you are an embodiment of thought as the 'me'. Now you say thought must continue because thought is going to enable me to fulfill myself, that thought will ultimately find the real. Is that not so? That is why you want thought to continue. You want thought to continue because you think thought is going to find the real, which you call happiness, God, or what you will.

Now, through the continuity of thought, do you find the real? To put it differently, does the thought process discover the real? Do you understand what I mean? I want happiness, and I search for it through various means—property, position, wealth, women, men, or whatever it be. All that is the demand of a thought for happiness, is it not? Now, can thought find happiness?

— 5 —

In Renewal, There Is No Death

So, our question is: Can there be a renewal, a regeneration, a freshness, a newness, through the continuity of the thought process? After all, if there is renewal, then we are not afraid of death. If for you there is renewal from moment to moment, there is no death. But there is death, and the fear of death, if you demand a continuity of the thought process.

— 6 —

Renewal by Ending the Thought Process

There is hope only when I see the truth that through continuity there is no renewal. And when I see that, what happens? Then I am only concerned with the ending of the thought process from moment to moment—which is not insanity!

— 7 —

Love Is Its Own Eternity

And when there is love, there is no death; there is death only when the thought process arises. When there is love, there is no death, because there is no fear; and love is not a continuous state—which is again the thought process. Love is merely being from moment to moment. Therefore, love is its own eternity.

— 8 —

Death and Immortality

In death we seek immortality; in the movement of birth and death we long for permanency; caught in the flux of time we crave for the timeless; being in shadow we believe in light. Death does not lead to immortality; there is immortality only in life without death. In life we know death for we cling to life. We gather, we become; because we gather, death comes, and knowing death, we cling to life.

The hope and belief in immortality is not the experiencing of immortality. Belief and hope must cease for the immortal to be. You the believer, the maker of desire, must cease for the immortal to be. Your very belief and hope strengthen the self...

— 9 —
The Present Is the Eternal

We do not understand life, the present, so we look to the future, to death...

The present is the eternal. Through time the timeless is not experienced. The now is ever existent; even if you escape into the future, the now is ever present.

— 10 —
Is There Enduring Joy?

Is there a possibility of finding enduring joy? There is, but to experience it there must be freedom. Without freedom, truth cannot be discovered, without freedom there can be no experience of the real. Freedom must be sought out— freedom from saviors, teachers, leaders; freedom from the self-enclosing walls of good and bad; freedom from authority and imitation; freedom from self, the cause of conflict and pain...

In the bliss of the real the experiencer and the experience cease. A mind-heart that is burdened with the memory of yesterday cannot live in the eternal present. Mind-heart must die each day for eternal being...

Die to your experience, to your memory. Die to your prejudice, pleasant or unpleasant. As you die there is the incorruptible; this is not a state of nothingness but of creative being. It is this renewal that will, if allowed, dissolve our problems and sorrows, however intricate and painful. Only in death of the self is there life.

— II —

The Fear of Death Is the Fear of Letting Go of What We Know

So, the self is a bundle of memories and nothing more. There is no spiritual entity as the 'me' or apart from the 'me' because when you say there is a spiritual entity apart from the 'me', it is still the product of thought; therefore, it is still within the field of thought, and thought is memory. So, the 'you', the 'me', the self—higher or lower, at whatever point it may be fixed—is memory...

What do we mean by death? Surely, a thing that is used constantly comes to an end; any machine that is constantly used wears out. Similarly, a body, being in constant use, comes to an end through disease, through accident, through age. That is inevitable—it may last a hundred or ten, but being used, it must wear out. We recognize and accept that because we see it happening continually.

— 12 —
The Known

So, you have no direct relationship with the unknown, and therefore you are afraid of death.

What do you know of life? Very little. You do not know your relationship to property, to your neighbor, to your wife, to ideas. You know only the superficial things, and you want to continue the superficial things. For God's sake, what a miserable life! Is not continuity a stupid thing?

— 13 —
Death and Life Are One

It is a stupid person that wants to continue—no man who understood the rich feelings of life would want continuity. When you understand life, you will find the unknown, for life is the unknown, and death and life are one. There is no division between life and death: it is the foolish and the ignorant who make the division, those who are concerned with their body and with their petty continuity. Such people use the theory of reincarnation as a means of covering up their fear, as a guarantee of their stupid little continuity. It is obvious that thought continues; but surely, a man who is seeking truth is not concerned with thought, for thought does not lead to truth. The theory of the 'me' continuing through reincarnation towards truth is a false idea, it is untrue. The 'me' is a bundle of memories, which is time, and the mere continuation of time does not lead you to the eternal, which is beyond time. The fear of death ceases only when the unknown enters your heart. Life is the unknown, as death is the unknown, as truth is the unknown.

— 14 —

Can We Let Go of the Self?:
Don't Miss the Whole Marvelous Show

Life is the unknown, sir; but we cling to one small expression of that life, and that which we cling to is merely memory, which is an incomplete thought; therefore, that which we cling to is unreal, it has no validity. The mind clings to that empty thing called memory, and memory is the mind, the self, at whatever level you like to fix it. So, mind, which is in the field of the known, can never invite the unknown. It is only when there is the unknown, a state of complete uncertainty, that there comes the cessation of fear and with it the perception of reality.

— 15 —

What Is God?

How are you going to find out? Are you going to accept somebody else's information? Or are you going to discover for yourself what God is?

CHAPTER EIGHT
Meditation Is Attention

— I —

Meditation Means to Pay Attention

Not to seek any form of psychological security, any form of gratification, requires investigation, constant watchfulness to see how the mind operates, and surely that is meditation, is it not? Meditation is not the practice of a formula or the repetition of certain words, which is all silly, immature. Without knowing the whole process of the mind, conscious as well as unconscious, any form of meditation is really a hindrance, an escape, a childish activity; it is a form of self-hypnosis. But to be aware of the process of thinking, to go into it carefully step by step with full consciousness and discover for oneself the ways of the self—that is meditation. It is only through self-knowledge that the mind can be free to discover what is truth, what is God, what is death, what is this thing that we call living.

— 2 —

Meditation Is Not Something Apart from Daily Living

Why is one lazy? Probably you are not eating rightly, you have worked too much, walked too much, talked too much, done so many things; and naturally the body, when it gets up in the morning, is lazy. Because you have not spent an intelligent day, the body is tired the next day. And it's no good disciplining the body. Whereas if you are attentive at the moment of your talking, when you are in your office—if you are completely attentive even for five minutes, that is enough. When you are eating, be attentive and do not eat fast, nor stuff yourself with all kinds of food. Then you will see that your body becomes, of itself, intelligent. You don't have to force it to be intelligent; it becomes intelligent, and that intelligence will tell it to get up or not to get up. So you begin to discover that one can live a life of going to the office and all the rest of it without this constant battle, because one has not wasted energy, but is using it totally all the time—and that is meditation.

— 3 —

Attention to the Whole Movement of
Relationship Is the Beginning of Meditation

You understand? Meditation is not what is done all the world over: repetition of words, sitting in a certain posture, breathing in a certain way, repeating some *sloka* or mantra over and over again. Naturally that makes the mind stupid, dull; and out of that stupidity, dullness, the mind becomes silent and you think you have got silence. That kind of meditation is merely self-hypnosis. It is not meditation at all. It is the most destructive way of meditating. But there is meditation which demands that you attend—attend to what you are saying to your wife, to your husband, to your children, how you talk to your servants if you have any, how you talk to your boss—be attentive at that moment, do not concentrate. Because concentration is something which is very ugly. Every schoolboy can do it because he is forced to do it. And you think that by forcing yourself to concentrate, you will get some peace. You won't. You will not have what you call "peace of mind"—you will have a piece of mind, which is not peace of mind. Concentration is an exclusion. When you want to concentrate on something, you are excluding, you are resisting, you are putting away things which you don't want. Whereas if you are attentive, then you can look at every thought, every movement; then there is no such thing as distraction, and then you can meditate.

— 4 —

Meditation Is Clarity

Then such meditation is a marvelous thing because it brings clarity. Meditation is clarity. Meditation then is silence, and that very silence is the disciplining process of life, not your disciplining yourself in order to achieve silence. But when you are attentive to every word, to every gesture, to all the things you are saying, feeling, to your motives, not correcting them, then out of that comes silence, and from that silence there is discipline. Then in that there is no effort; there is a movement which is not of time at all. And such a human being is a joyous person; he does not create enmity, he does not bring unhappiness.

— 5 —

Meditation, Not Collective Thought, Understands
Life: Be Your Own Light

Truth is something that cannot be given to you. You have to find it out for yourself. And to find it out for yourself, you must be a law to yourself, you must be a guide to yourself, not the political man that is going to save the world, not the communist, not the leader, not the priest, not the sannyasi, not the books; you have to live, you have to be a law to yourself. And therefore no authority—which means completely standing alone, not outwardly, but inwardly completely

alone, which means no fear. And when the mind has understood the nature of fear, the nature of death, and that
extraordinary thing called love, then it has understood, not
verbalized, not thought about, but actually lived. Then out
of that understanding comes a mind that is active, but completely still. This whole process of understanding life, of
freeing oneself from all the battles, not in some future, but
immediately, giving your whole attention to it—all that is
meditation: not sitting in some corner and holding your nose
and repeating some silly words, mesmerizing yourself, that
is not meditation at all, that is self-hypnosis. But to understand life, to be free from sorrow—actually, not verbally, not
theoretically, but actually—to be free of fear and of death
brings about a mind that is completely still. And all that is
meditation.

— 6 —

Meditation Is Self-Knowledge

Meditation is self-knowledge and without self-knowledge
there is no meditation. If you are not aware of all your responses all the time, if you are not fully conscious, fully
cognizant of your daily activities, merely to lock yourself in
a room and sit down in front of a picture of your guru, of
your Master, to meditate, is an escape, because without self-
knowledge there is no right thinking and, without right
thinking, what you do has no meaning, however noble your

intentions are. Thus prayer has no significance without self-knowledge but when there is self-knowledge there is right thinking and hence right action.

— 7 —

Meditation Is Emptying the Mind of the Past

Meditation, then, is emptying the mind of the past, not as an idea, not as an ideology which you are going to practice day after day—to empty the mind of the past. Because the man or the entity who empties the mind of the past is the result of the past. But to understand this whole structure of the mind, which is the result of the past, and to empty the mind of the past demands a deep awareness. To be aware of your conditioning, your way of talking, your gestures, the callousness, the brutality, the violence, just to be aware of it without condemning it—then out of that awareness comes a state of mind which is completely quiet. To understand this quietness, the silence of the mind, you must understand sorrow, because most of us live in sorrow; whether we are aware of it or not, we have never put an end to sorrow; it is like our shadow, it is with us night and day.

— 8 —

In the Still Mind Is Bliss

In sorrow there is a great deal of self-pity, concern with one's own loneliness, emptiness; and when one becomes aware of that emptiness, loneliness, there is self-pity, and that self-pity we call sorrow. So as long as there is sorrow, conscious or unconscious, within the mind, there is no quietness of the mind, there is no stillness of the mind. The stillness of the mind comes where there is beauty and love; you cannot separate beauty from love. Beauty is not an ornament, nor good taste. It does not lie in the line of the hills, nor in architecture. There is beauty when you know what love is, and you cannot possibly know what love is when there is not intelligence, austerity, and order. And nobody can give this to you, no saint, no god, no mahatma—nobody! No authority in the world can give it to you. You as a human being have to understand this whole structure—the structure and the nature of your life of every day, what you do, what you think, what your motives are, how you behave, how you are caught in your own conclusions, in your own conditioning. It must begin there, in daily life, and if you cannot alter that totally, completely, bring about a total mutation in yourself, you will never know that still mind. And it is only the still mind that can find out: it is only the still mind that knows what truth is. Because that still mind *has* no imagination; it does not project its desires; it is a still mind—and it is only then that there is the bliss of something that cannot be put into words.

— 9 —

When You Are Eating, Eat

Questioner: I feel that my daily life is unimportant, that I should be doing something else.

Krishnamurti: When you are eating, eat. When you are going for a walk, walk. Don't say, "I must be doing something else." When you are reading, give your attention completely to that, whether it is a detective novel, a magazine, the Bible, or what you will. The complete attention is a complete action, and therefore there is no "I must be doing something else..."

What is important is not what we are doing but whether we can give total attention.

— 10 —

In Stillness, Problems Are Resolved:
The Cup Is Useful Only when It Is Empty

Questioner: You are advocating that we liquidate the environment within us. Why do you advocate that? What is the use of it?

Krishnamurti: I am not advocating anything. But you know, the cup is useful only when it is empty. With most of us, the mind is clouded, cluttered up with so many things—pleasant and unpleasant experiences, knowledge, patterns or formulas of behavior, and so on. It is never empty. And creation can take place only in the mind that is totally empty...

I don't know if you have ever noticed what sometimes happens when you have a problem, either mathematical or psychological. You think about it a great deal, you worry over it like a dog chewing on a bone, but you can't find an answer. Then you let it alone, you go away from it, you take a walk; and suddenly, out of that emptiness, comes the answer. Now, how does this take place? Your mind has been very active within its own limitations about that problem, but you have not found the answer, so you have put the problem aside. Then your mind becomes somewhat quiet, somewhat still, empty; and in that stillness, that emptiness, the problem is resolved. Similarly, when one dies each minute to the inward environment, to the inward commitments, to the inward memories, to the inward secrecies and agonies, there is then an emptiness in which alone a new thing can take place.

— II —

The Still Mind

And it is only a very still mind, not a disciplined mind, that has understood and therefore is free. It is only that still mind that can know what is creation. Because the word *God* has been spoiled...

But to find out that something which is beyond time, you must have a very still mind. And that still mind is not a dead mind but is tremendously active; anything that is moving at the highest speed and is active is always quiet. It is only the dull mind that worries about that is anxious, fearful. Such a mind can never be still. And it is only a mind that is still that is a religious mind. And it is only the religious mind that can find out, or be in that state of creation. And it is only such a mind that can bring about peace in the world. And that peace is your responsibility, the responsibility of each one of us, not the politician, not the soldier, not the lawyer, not the businessman, not the communist, socialist, nobody. It is your responsibility, how you live, how you live your daily life. If you want peace in the world, you have to live peacefully, not hating each other, not being envious, not seeking power, not pursuing competition. Because out of that freedom from these, you have love. It is only a mind that is capable of loving that will know what it is to live peacefully.

Sources

Abbreviation of Titles by J. Krishnamurti
Referred to in Source Notes

CL: *Commentaries on Living*, Series I, II, III, Quest Books,
       1967. Copyright 1956, KFA.

CW: *The Collected Works of J. Krishnamurti, 1933-1967.*
       First published by Kendall-Hunt, 1991-92.
       Copyright 1991/1992, KFA.

ESL: *Education and the Significance of Life*,
       HarperSanFrancisco, 1981. Copyright 1953, KFA.

FLF: *The First and Last Freedom*, HarperSanFrancisco,
       1975. Copyright 1954, KFA.

LA: *Life Ahead*, Harper & Row, 1975. Copyright 1963,
       KFA.

ML: *Meeting Life*, HarperSanFrancisco, 1991. Copyright
       1991, KFT, Ltd.

TTT: *Think on These Things*, HarperPerennial, 1989.
       Copyright 1964, KFA.

— Sources —

SECTION ONE

Chapter One
1. CW, Vol. 8, p. 146
2. Ibid
3. Ibid, p. 147
4. FLF, Chap. 9, p. 76
5. CW, Vol. 5, pp. 334-5
6. FLF, Chap. 3, pp. 36-7
7. CW, Vol. 5, p. 80
8. CW, Vol. 5, pp. 30-1
9. ESL, Chap. 2, pp. 43-4
10. FLF, Chap. 16, pp. 112-13

Chapter Two
1. FLF, Chap. 2, pp. 28-9
2. CW, Vol. 7, p. 101
3. CW, Vol. 8, pp. 117-18
4. Ibid, p. 118
5. Ibid, p. 119
6. CW, Vol. 15, p. 31
7. Ibid, p. 31
8. CW, Vol. 17, p. 182

Chapter Three
1. CW, Vol. 4, pp. 196-7
2. FLF, Chap. 5, p. 53
3. CW, Vol. 16, p. 168
4. Ibid, p. 167
5. Ibid
6. CW, Vol. 16, p. 55
7. Ibid
8. CW, Vol. 15, p. 66
9. Ibid, pp. 65-6

10. CW, Vol. 15, p. 32
11. CW, Vol. 9, p. 35
12. CW, Vol. 4, p. 180
13. CW, Vol. 11, p. 337

Chapter Four
1. CW, Vol. 1, p. 115
2. CW, Vol. 9, p. 35
3. CW, Vol. 5, p. 214
4. CW, Vol. 2, p. 98
5. CW, Vol. 11, p. 34
6. ESL, Chap. 3, p. 55
7. Ibid, pp. 55-7
8. Ibid, pp. 64-7

Chapter Five
1. CW, Vol. 17, p. 167; CW, Vol. 15, p. 275
2. CW, Vol. 8, p. 135
3. CL, Series I, Chap. 27, p. 64
4. Ibid, pp. 64-5
5. CW, Vol. 5, p. 216
6. CW, Vol. 15, p. 164
7. Ibid
8. Ibid, p. 167
9. CW, Vol. 17, pp. 180-1
10. Ibid

Chapter Six
1. CW, Vol. 5, p. 50
2. CW, Vol. 15, p. 303
3. CW, Vol. 15, p. 307
4. CW, Vol. 16, pp. 152-3

Chapter Seven
1. CW, Vol. 8, pp. 152-3
2. CW, Vol. 5, pp. 19-20
3. CW, Vol. 8, p. 121
4. CW, Vol. 15, p. 49
5. FLF, Question 36, pp. 280-1

SECTION TWO

Chapter One
1. CW, Vol. 17, p. 161
2. Ibid
3. Ibid, pp. 161-2
4. Ibid, p. 162
5. Ibid
6. Ibid
7. Ibid, p. 163
8. Ibid, p. 164
9. Ibid, p. 165
10. CW, Vol. 3, p. 225

Chapter Two
1. CL, Series I, Chap. 30, p. 70
2. Ibid, pp. 70-1
3. Ibid, p. 71
4. Ibid
5. CW, Vol. 12, p. 246
6. CW, Vol. 3, p. 203
7. Ibid, p. 154
8. Ibid, pp. 154-5
9. CW, Vol. 17, p. 255
10. Ibid
11. Ibid, pp. 255-6
12. Ibid, p. 256
13. Ibid, p. 258
14. CW, Vol. 9, p. 86
15. Ibid
16. Ibid, pp. 86-7

Chapter Three
1. CW, Vol. 5, pp. 251-2
2. Ibid, p. 252
3. Ibid
4. CL, Series II, Chap. 6, pp. 20-22
5. Ibid, p. 22

Chapter Four
1. CW, Vol. 17, p. 185
2. Ibid, pp. 185-6
3. Ibid, p. 186
4. Ibid
5. Ibid
6. CL, Series III, Chap. 55, pp. 302-3
7. Ibid, p. 303
8. Ibid
9. CW, Vol. 7, pp. 214-15
10. CW, Vol. 15, p. 226

Chapter Five
1. CL, Series I, Chap. 56, pp. 141-2
2. Ibid, p. 142
3. CL, Series II, Chap. 53, pp. 224-5
4. Ibid, pp. 225-6
5. CL, Series III, Chap. 23, p. 110
6. Ibid, pp. 110-11

7. Ibid, pp. 111-12
8. Ibid, p. 112

Chapter Six
1. CW, Vol. 7, p. 40
2. CW, Vol. 15, p. 16
3. Ibid, pp. 16-17
4. Ibid, p. 17
5. CW, Vol. 9, p. 82
6. CW, Vol. 15, p. 166
7. Ibid, pp. 166-7
8. CW, Vol. 12, p. 244

Chapter Seven
1. CL, Series I, Chap. 57, p. 146
2. Ibid
3. CW, Vol. 17, pp. 234-5
4. CW, Vol. 7, p. 83
5. LA, Pt. 1, pp. 66-7
6. Ibid
7. CW, Vol. 7, p. 84
8. CW, Vol. 17, pp. 182-3
9. Ibid, p. 183
10. ESL, Chap. 2, pp. 43-4
11. Ibid, p. 44

Chapter Eight
1. CW, Vol. 8, p. 198
2. Ibid
3. CW, Vol. 7, p. 236
4. Ibid
5. CW, Vol. 6, p. 238
6. Ibid, p. 237
7. FLF, Question 6, p. 166
8. Ibid, pp. 166-7

9. From a talk given in Mumbai (Bombay), India, 21 March 1948
10. FLF, Question 8, pp. 172-3
11. Ibid, p. 173
12. CW, Vol. 9, pp. 88-9
13. Ibid, p. 89
14. Ibid
15. Ibid
16. Ibid

Chapter Nine
1. CW, Vol. 9, p. 96
2. Ibid, pp. 96-7
3. CW, Vol. 9, p. 97
4. Ibid, p. 98
5. Ibid
6. Ibid, pp. 98-9
7. Ibid, p. 100

SECTION THREE

Chapter One
1. ESL, Chap. 2, pp. 17-18
2. Ibid, p. 18
3. Ibid, pp. 18-19
4. ESL, Chap. 1, pp. 15-16
5. ESL, Chap. 5, p. 83
6. Ibid, pp. 83-4
7. CW, Vol. 8, pp. 157-8
8. CW, Vol. 15, pp. 13-14

Chapter Two
1. CW, Vol. 8, p. 73
2. CW, Vol. 7, p. 303

3. Ibid, p. 303-4
4. Ibid, p. 304
5. CW, Vol. 6, p. 326
6. Ibid
7. CW, Vol. 8, p. 252

Chapter Three
1. TTT, Chap. 7, p. 53
2. Ibid, pp. 53-4
3. LA, Introduction, p. 21
4. LA, Pt. 2, p. 163
5. Ibid, pp. 163-4
6. From a talk given in Mumbai (Bombay), India, 28 March 1948
7. Ibid
8. CW, Vol. 5, p. 62
9. Ibid, pp. 144-5
10. TTT, Chap. 17, p. 147

Chapter Four
1. CW, Vol. 15, p. 303
2. CL, Series I, Chap. 41, pp. 99-100
3. Ibid, p. 100
4. Ibid, pp. 101-2
5. ML, pp. 118-19
6. CW, Vol. 7, p. 73
7. LA, Pt. 1, pp. 114-15
8. LA, Pt. 1, p. 137
9. Ibid, Chap. 19, p. 138
10. FLF, Chap. 16, p. 111
11. LA, Pt. 1, p. 141
12. LA, Pt. 2, p. 177

SECTION FOUR

Chapter One
1. CW, Vol. 17, p. 7
2. CW, Vol. 3, pp. 159-60
3. Ibid, p. 160
4. Ibid
5. Ibid
6. CW, Vol. 5, p. 212
7. Ibid
8. CW, Vol. 8, p. 344
9. CW, Vol. 16, p. 45
10. Ibid, p. 46
11. Ibid
12. CW, Vol. 12, p. 246

Chapter Two
1. CW, Vol. 8, p. 337
2. Ibid
3. Ibid, p. 338
4. CW, Vol. 6, pp. 129-30
5. Ibid, p. 129
6. CW, Vol. 16, p. 215

Chapter Three
1. CW, Vol. 15, p. 43
2. Ibid
3. CW, Vol. 7, pp. 88-9
4. CL, Series II, Chap. 25, pp. 111-12
5. Ibid, p. 112

Chapter Four
1. CW, Vol. 5, p. 142
2. Ibid

3. Ibid
4. Ibid, pp. 142-3

Chapter Five
1. CW, Vol. 5, pp. 147-8
2. Ibid, p. 149
3. Ibid
4. CL, Series I, Chap. 17, pp. 40-1
5. Ibid, pp. 41-2
6. Ibid, p. 42
7. CW, Vol. 5, p. 197
8. Ibid, p. 99
9. CW, Vol. 6, pp. 42-3
10. CW, Vol. 4, p. 177
11. CW, Vol. 5, pp. 216-17
12. CW, Vol. 4, p. 210
13. CW, Vol. 12, p. 134
14. From a talk given in Chennai (Madras), India, 28 December 1947
15. CW, Vol. 5, p. 175

Chapter Six
1. CW, Vol. 14, p. 95
2. CW, Vol. 11, p. 251
3. CW, Vol. 15, p. 69
4. Ibid

Chapter Seven
1. CW, Vol. 5, p. 67
2. Ibid
3. Ibid, pp. 67-8
4. Ibid, p. 68
5. Ibid
6. Ibid, p. 69

7. Ibid
8. CW, Vol. 4, p. 13
9. Ibid, p. 12
10. CW, Vol. 4, pp. 49-50
11. CW, Vol. 5, p. 125
12. Ibid, p. 127
13. Ibid
14. Ibid
15. LA, Pt. 1, p. 45

Chapter Eight
1. CW, Vol. 8, p. 255
2. CW, Vol. 17, p. 124
3. Ibid
4. Ibid, pp. 124-5
5. CW, Vol. 15, p. 322
6. FLF, Question 19, p. 220
7. CW, Vol. 17, p. 242
8. Ibid
9. CW, Vol. 16, p. 246
10. CW, Vol. 15, pp. 245-6
11. CW, Vol. 15, pp. 322-3

Resources:
Schools and Foundations

— The Krishnamurti Schools —

INDIA

Rishi Valley Education Centre
Boarding School (Ages 9 to 18)
Rishi Valley Post
Chittoor District, 517 352, A.P.
email: rishivalley_mpl@yahoo.com

Rajghat Education Centre
Boarding School (Ages 7 to 18)
Rajghat Fort
Varanasi 221 001, U.P.
www.jkrishnamurti.org
email: admin@jkrishnamurti.org

U.K.

Brockwood Park School
International Boarding School (From age 14)
Bramdean, Near Alresford
Hampshire SO24 0LQ, U.K.
www.brockwood.org.uk
email: admin@brockwood.org.uk

U.S.A.

Oak Grove School
Day School (Ages 3 to 18), Boarding (9 to19)
220 West Lomita Avenue
Ojai, CA 93023
www.oakgroveschool.com
email: office@oakgroveschool.com
Admissions: enroll@oakgroveschool.com

— Krishnamurti Foundations —

U.S.A.

Krishnamurti Foundation of America
P.O. Box 1560
Ojai, CA 93024, U.S.A.
Tel: (805) 646-2726
Fax: (805) 646-6674
www.kfa.org
email: kfa@kfa.org

CANADA

Krishnamurti Educational Centre
538 Swanwick Road, R.R. 1
Victoria, B.C. V9C 3Y8, CANADA
Tel: (250) 474-1488
Fax: (250) 474-1104
email: namurti@islandnet.com

U.K.

Krishnamurti Foundation Trust, Ltd.
Brockwood Park
Bramdean
Hampshire, SO24 0LQ, U.K.
Tel: [44] (0) (1962) 771-525
Fax [44] (0) (1962) 771-159
email: info@brockwood.org.uk

INDIA

Krishnamurti Foundation India
Vasanta Vihar
64-65 Greenways Road
Chennai 600 028, INDIA
Tel: [91] (44) 493-7803/7596
Fax: [91] (44) 499-1360
email: kfihq@md2.vsnl.net.in

LATIN AMERICA

Fundación Krishnamurti Latino Americana
Alfonso Esteban, Secretary
c/o Juan Perez Almeida 12 2° A
28019 Madrid, SPAIN
email: fkl.ae@mibbva.com

Index

Recommended Reading

Talks with American Students
Most of us in this confused and
brutal world try to carve out a
private life of our own, a life in
which we can be happy and
peaceful and yet live with the
things of this world. $9.95. 182 pp.
ISBN 0-87773-021-0. Shambhala

A Flame of Learning:
Krishnamurti with Teachers
At Brockwood Park, England, a
school dedicated to imparting
Krishnamurti's teachings as part
of the curriculum, the following
questions are addressed in the six
dialogues: What is the meaning of
freedom and authority? Is it
possible to have no motive or self-
interest in action? $17.95. 205 pp.
ISBN 90-6271-829-9. Mirananda

The First and Last Freedom

The First and Last Freedom is an incredibly profound publication. Krishnamurti's powerfully insightful words resonate with affection and wisdom, "Love is love, not to be defined or described by the mind as exclusive or inclusive. Love is its own eternity: it is the real, the supreme, the immeasurable." $15.00. 288 pp. ISBN 0-06-064831-7. HarperCollins

Think on These Things

This is the most popular Krishnamurti book. It is a series of talks and questions-and-answers with students and teachers from the Krishnamurti schools in India. This book comes with a complete index of all the questions presented to Krishnamurti. Some of them include: What is shyness? What is jealousy? What is happiness in life? and, Why do we cry, and what is sorrow? $13.00. 258 pp. ISBN 0-06-091609-5. HarperCollins

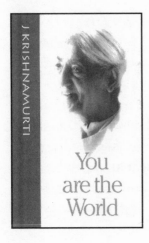

You are the World
This volume consists of talks Krishnamurti gave at four well-known California universities: Brandeis, Berkeley, Stanford, and UCSC. Sensing the urge for freedom in his audience, he directs their attention away from superficial change—at the same time challenging the Western dialectical tradition—and towards that inward revolution which can only come about when, as Krishnamurti says, "you are the world." $9.99. 164 pp. ISBN 81-87326-02-6. KFI

Commentaries on Living: I, II, III
This is a wonderful series of books written by Krishnamurti. Many of Krishnamurti's books are compilations of his talks around the world; however, Krishnamurti was encouraged by his friend Aldous Huxley to write, which lead to *Commentaries On Living*—a masterpiece for us to read. $13.00. Series I, 254 pp. ISBN 0-8356-0390-3. Quest Books

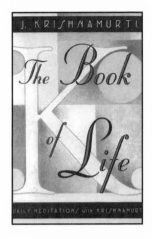

The Book of Life

The Book of Life presents passages from Krishnamurti's talks and writings on a different theme for every week of the year. The subjects embrace far-ranging topics as self-knowledge, desire, sorrow, death and meditation. There are 365 timeless daily mediations, developed thematically, illuminating the concepts of freedom, personal transformation, living fully awake, and much more. $16.00. 228pp. ISBN 0-06-250526-2. HarperCollins

The Mirror of Relationship

This Study Book features statements on this theme from Krishnamurti's talks and discussions held between 1933 and 1967. They have proven helpful in dialogues and for use in high school and college classrooms. He says, "if you deny sexuality, then you must close your eyes, cut out your tongue, put out your eyes, and never look at anything—the first thing is not to condemn, and then you will know what love is." $10.95. 134pp. ISBN 1-888004-05-3. KPA

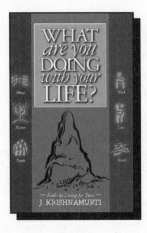

Copies of *What Are You Doing with Your Life?* and other books, cassettes, videos, and CDs may be ordered through Krishnamurti Publications of America. For a current Catalogue of Publications, contact KPA at:

Krishnamurti Publications of America
(A division of Krishnamurti Foundation of America)
P.O. Box 1560
Ojai, California 93024-1560
(805) 646-2726

www.kfa.org
You may visit our web site and online bookstore at any hour, place an order within minutes and have the items delivered to your front door—even if you live on the other side of the planet. Please note that you will find a wider selection of items listed on KFA's online bookstore than in our printed retail catalogue. Log on and check us out today!